Perilous Return

D.M.Doolan

Published in 2024 by FeedARead.com Publishing

A CIP catalogue record for this title is available from the British Library.

One

After a while, the force made her stumble and fall, she picked herself up and continued to look around her petrified. Soon she realised the danger she was in and began to look for an escape. Climbing trees was her solution to other dangers in her life. Often she vanished from the path of a great beast by scaling a tree, but this time the trees were falling around her – they were being convulsed too.

"Anika!" she heard the call through the destruction around her, "Anika!"

She found her voice, "Papa!" she yelled with all her might.

"Anika!" the final call before the voice was drowned out by an almighty roar. When she looks back on this day, she remembers it was the roar that brought overwhelming fear racing through her body. The wall of water that pounded towards her after that was a second thought, one that destroyed everything she loved and lived for but didn't hold a memory of being as terrifying.

"Papa," she whispered now, holding out her arms in the direction the sound had come from before her small body was whisked up in a churn of freezing water and carried along. Swimming was not a skill anyone thought it necessary to teach, so she fell below the water again and again as she frantically fought for breath. It quickly dawned on her that the mighty waters, as her Papa called it could kill her. Her people used these waters – they fished from them but few had the life-saving skill of being able to swim. All around her various things bobbed above and below the water – she was not alone. A small amount of fascination eclipsed her fear as she watched a Woolly Mammoth struggle to stay above the water just metres from where she was. Huge chunks of ice swirled around and came precariously close to her. As the force of the wave submerged her once again, she almost gave in to the notion that it was her choice when she died. She only needs to open her mouth and the water would flood into her lungs and she could leave this earth. Maybe she could be with her Papa again. It seemed like hours as the decision loomed in her mind, but it was taken away from her when she rose above the surface once again. Finally, she saw a chance of survival. Close to her was a tree trunk, still with smaller branches and leaves attached. She reached for it but it rolled out of her hands, so she kicked her feet and leapt out of the water landing with a thud, stomach first on top of the tree trunk. She thought her weight may sink it but after a bob or two, it settled on the top, floating along oblivious to the devastation around it. Landing on her stomach had winded her and she struggled for air, but eventually, her breath returned and she just lay there, hands grasping the rough bark. After a while, she stopped attempting to see where the water was taking her and she put her head sideways onto the trunk. The bark of the tree scratched her face but exhaustion finally overtook her, her eyes began to close as the tumultuous wave turned into a smooth running river before finally coming to a stop ten miles from where the earth had begun to shake. She was all alone.

Two

It was a long time before Anika awoke. When she did, she lifted her head slowly from the trunk which had come to rest amongst the tall grass. A slight wind blew her mud-caked hair across her face.

"Papa," she said quietly. She sat up and looked around her, while muddy water lapped her toes making her realise her shoes were now gone. *Papa will be mad*, she thought, considering he had only finished making them a few nights before. He pretended to be cross at how fast her feet were growing and the number of animals he had to catch, skin and thread together to create new shoes for her.

The air was warm and as she looked at the sun she realised it was nearly midday. All of a sudden, her stomach gave a loud growl. She wondered how long it had been since she had eaten. Slowly, she stood up. Her side ached as she lifted her tunic and saw a nasty gash that had bled and was now starting to dry up. In haste, she looked around her. It looked like home or where they were settled at the moment. Like all people, they moved around a lot, settling where there was food then moving on when food diminished. Summer was the period they stayed in one place for a long length of time. Further inland where the bushes were ripe and roots were plentiful. In winter, they always went closer to the coastal lands where the mighty waters were. Even though they were in the middle of summer now, her father had decided they should go on a trip. Leaving their settlement behind for a few days, they had headed to the sea so her father could continue teaching her to fish. Unusually, he had introduced her to many tasks that were normally considered to be for boys only, but he had no sons and wanted her to be able to take care of herself when he was no longer there. That's where they had been when the earth had begun to shake. Well, where she had been. Father had gone back into the forest to hunt for breakfast. The thought of her father and hearing his voice just before the wild waters had swept her away, made her want to cry. Swallowing hard, the lump in her throat hurt as she forced it back down. *Survivors have no time for crying*, she heard her father's voice.

Forcing her feet to move, she stepped over the trunk and into the grass before entering a wood where the water wasn't as deep but had moistened the ground considerably. The wind blew through the trees and made the branches sway back and forth. Until the ground felt harder under her feet, she carried on walking. Her feet were used to hard surfaces as she spent most of the day barefoot only putting on her shoes when long journeys called for it. Spotting a small collection of rocks she walked over and began to dig in the earth beneath the shade of them. When she reached the damp earth beneath, she removed some and, lifting her tunic, applied it to the gash on her side as her father had shown her. Even in her short life, she knew that infection could kill, she had seen it at least twice. She sat on the rock and remembered the day she had seen her father's brother trampled by a Woolly Rhinoceros. It had been the feast of the longest day and, as tradition commanded, the men had planned and carried out a great hunt. This meant they had to kill one of the larger animals found in their vicinity. The choice was normally between Woolly Mammoth, Rhinoceros, Giant Elk, or Antelope. This particular time they had spotted a group of Rhinos on the plateau just above the valley. Through careful planning, they had managed to entrap one of them between a forest and a river using the one thing all animals feared, fire. Anika had only heard the story but remembers them bringing him home. Her father had carried his brother for miles over his shoulders and he had been placed in front of all the medicine women in their tribe. None could stop the infection that spread across his body from the wound on his leg. It took him three days to die and in absolute agony. *No,* she thought as she checked the wound again, *she wouldn't die that way.*

All of a sudden, she heard a noise behind her. She was used to being surprised by animals in the world she lived in but she wasn't used to being unarmed against them. Standing without a stick, slingshot, spear or axe she was frightened. *If you can't fight, hide,* she heard her father's voice and swiftly crouched behind a bush blooming with lush berries. Closely she watched, through a gap in the bramble and saw a Giant Elk meandering through the trees. She saw from the fact it had antlers that it was a male and she knew that by the end of summer their antlers would be rock solid and of great use to make weapons and tools. It seemed to be alone which was unusual but maybe he was in search of a female pack ready for mating.

If only father was here, Anika thought. Her father was a great hunter, renowned amongst the tribe and had been known to tackle a Giant Elk on his own. However, Anika was a slim, slender child of no more than eight years she believed as her Papa was unsure of her actual year of birth he just knew the approximate amount of seasons that had passed since. Unsurprisingly, he didn't like to talk about it as her birth had been the cause of her mother's death. Not that he ever suggested it like that, she was merely a baby coming into the world – it wasn't her fault. But, her blood loss had been too great and the medicine women of the area couldn't save her so the greater forces chose to take her. It wasn't unusual, Anika knew, to die during childbirth – it was a perilous position to put yourself in and she couldn't understand why women did it. Her father had tried to explain it to her once, but she had found it all a bit disgusting and decided not to listen properly.

Standing perfectly still, the Giant Elk was smelling the air. It had sensed her and was contemplating its next move. Finally, it came to a decision and leapt over a bush to its left before crashing through the woods and disappearing from view. Anika sat down on her bottom with a sigh of relief. She knew that that great beast, more than three times her height, could easily crush her or impale her on its antlers. Lifting her head, she once again viewed the lush berries right in front of her. And once again, her belly rumbled as a reminder that it needed filling. You never wasted an opportunity to eat and if you came across food you seized it, either for immediate sustenance or for later use. As Anika had no way of carrying or storing food at present, she decided to shovel as many as she could into her mouth until her stomach was bloated and red juice dripped down her chin. Satisfied, she sat back and after a moment's reprieve, she set to contemplating her next move.

I need to get back to father, she thought, *I'm not ready to survive on my own.*

Throughout her short life, her father had been meticulous with his teaching, but there were many things she still didn't know that meant she wasn't ready to live alone. Many times over the years she had seen older children go off into the wild, as their tribe commanded, to prove they were ready for adulthood. In this time, they had to live alone, surviving off the land, finding or building shelter and returning with goods the tribe could use. The length of time these youngsters were expected to be alone varied and was dependant on the season, their skills and their attitude towards the task. Most had passed through at least forty seasons before they were ready to take on this tribal challenge. Some never returned and their parents suffered the shame of producing a child that couldn't contribute to the survival of their people. Sons were considered to be of higher prestige although many daughters had proven their worth over past years. Besides, the tribe couldn't continue without them.

In general, male and female were treated equally and decisions were made together as a group. If a decision couldn't be made, the overall choice of the tribe's next step normally came down to the leader (who was always a man).

Anika thought about her journey. She knew if she followed the retreating water eventually she would find her father, but how far she had travelled she didn't know. It had been early evening when the earth had started to tremble and she had woken at midday which she could only assume was the day after. *What if I had been asleep longer than a day?* She questioned herself. She remembered once a young boy in her tribe had fallen from some rocks and cracked his head on the floor beneath. The medicine women had brought out the bruise and lump beneath with one of their concoctions, but he had stayed asleep for four whole days before he had awoken finally with no memory of what had occurred.

Shaking her head to regain her concentration, she stood up and walked back to the tree trunk she had come from. Already, she noticed the water was shallower than before. If she didn't start following it now, there would be nothing left to follow. It worried her being out in the open like this with little protection, but she didn't think she had any other choice. So off she went, trudging through the sodden ground, round broken trees and twisted bracken, which made the journey harder, but she made some progress and had covered about three miles by the time the sun began to set. This was the time of day that frightened her the most. A shelter was an absolute necessity she knew so she began to look around her for such a place. Leaving the clear path of the retreating water made her wary and she chose not to go too far. However, after a thirty-minute traipse through the woods she spotted the perfect place. It involved her climbing up a small cliff but the roots from the trees above allowed for this and she was a great climber. As she neared the top, she ensured she made a lot of noise in the hope of flushing out any wild animal that lived in or around the space she wanted to use. She waited, nothing moved. She clambered over the lip of the cliff and rested on her elbows. Slowly, she lifted her head.

“AAAHHHHHHH!!!” she yelled at the top of her voice, before once again hiding low and flat. Again, nothing moved, no sound could be heard except the low whistle of the wind through the trees and the occasional chirp of a settling bird.

Lightly on her feet, she walked towards the cave. After a brief observation of the cave entrance, she was satisfied that it wasn’t being used by a large beast and she began to look around for wood to start her fire. Man’s advantage over animals. From almost as soon as she had proper control over her hands, her father had taught her to make fire. Without it, it was difficult to survive and almost impossible to thrive. She worked speedily now, placing the parts she had found into their piles. A small pile of tinder consisting of bone-dry dead grass, dandelion fluff and old stalks. Next was her kindling pile with slightly larger sticks fallen from the trees around her. For her base, she found a piece of Elm bark and she began the lengthy process of using friction to create an ember. Having repeatedly started fires every day since about her tenth season she knew the speed, rotation and force needed to create that essential ember. As it glowed, she added thin pieces of tinder and blew. When lit, smoke surrounded her and she began to pile smaller pieces on top. Before long, her fire was raging and she continued to add larger branches to ensure it was extensive enough to protect her through the night, whilst also ensuring the area around it wasn't flammable so it didn't spread unwanted.

After this, she set about finding something more substantial than berries to eat. When collecting firewood she had noticed many holes created by hares in the area, so she grabbed a flaming branch off the fire and approached one such hole. Thrusting the branch into the hole she knew the lack of air would put out the flame and create a smoke that would drift around the hare hole forcing the creatures to come out. Hoping it would choose this hole rather than the many others connected to this tunnel, she continued to hold it for a few more seconds. Removing the branch, she waited, crouching on her toes. Narrowly missing the first one that darted past her at an astounding speed, she was pleased when a second appeared just after more cautiously and she took the moment to grasp it. Killing the animal without a knife of sorts was more difficult and gutting it was near impossible. After ensuring it was dead, she placed it down close to the fire to ensure other predators didn't come near it then she went in search of a sharp stone to help her gut it and remove the skin. At this point, her luck ran out and the stone she finally found made the job difficult and it took her way into the night before she eventually produced a hare ready for cooking. However, when your belly was only full of tangy berries the meat from the hare (normally tough) tasted succulent and kept her full through the night. It passed without any disturbances and as she drifted off to sleep lying on a bed of fresh leaves she could have sworn she heard her father calling her name.

Three

Watching through the bushes, he saw her light the fire and smoke out the hare and watched her closely as she lay down and fell asleep amongst the leaves. Only once he thought she was asleep did he leave her. It was a short walk back to where his people were at present. Arriving only weeks ago, they were still in the process of setting up their camp. Many of the tribe had begun to put together wooden shelters where three poles met in the middle and were tied together using sinew or animal hair that someone had painstakingly bound together to strengthen. Over this they would either place branches until the gaps were filled then cover them with leaves to rainproof it or, if they were lucky enough, the roof would be made of animal skin. Some houses would have a hole in the top to allow smoke out. The ones that didn't would place their fire just outside the entrance. Walking across the clearing he viewed the trees around their space and the hills that surrounded them.

"Papa," he called as he entered his temporary shelter, "Papa," he waited for his eyes to adjust then saw his father in the corner, sat on an animal hide and shaping a tool of some kind.

"Yes, son," he said with a smile as he saw his oldest child silhouetted against the entrance to his tent.

"I was in the forest earlier," he began.

"Which way?" his father interrupted.

He thought about it for a while, remembering where the sun had set that evening. "To the East," he said whilst lifting his hand and pointing in that direction.

His father nodded his head but carried on with his task.

"Well, I was up in the forest and I saw flames so I went to see what it was." He sat down on the hide beside his father whose attention had now been grasped by this revelation.

"A person," his father said, more as a statement than a question.

"Yes, a girl. Young she was. No more than eight collections of seasons I think." He counted on his fingers, "maybe seven." He looked again, holding up his fingers. "That is seven, yes father?"

Chuckling, his father looked up. "Yes son, but you should know your numbers to ten by now and higher even. Remember the notches on the stick, we went higher than ten last time." He rooted around in his bag sat next to him on the mat. It was, like everything, made of animal skin and had been sewn together using a flint needle and sinew from an animal's insides. Out of it, he pulled a long thick piece of wood that had notches made in it all the way along.

"Dad, dad, not now. I need to tell you about the girl," he pleaded.

"Ok, ok, carry on. Who was with her?" he questioned.

"No one, that's the thing, She was completely alone."

At this, his father rose – ensuring he stood in the middle of the shelter so as not to hit his head on the surrounding branches.

"Alone? That's not right. She'll be eaten alive out here," he said, remembering the herd of mammoth he had seen in the valley some days before and the remains of a deer that had been torn limb from limb by what he suspected was a cave lion. It was an area brimming with food ready for hunting but a small child out here alone wouldn't have a chance, no matter her skills.

"Dad, what are you thinking?" the boy asked as he watched his father scratch his beard covering the whole of his chin. His hair was black and his skin tanned from the summer sun. Dark brown eyes sat close together on his face and were almost concealed by the curly hairs of his fringe hanging down over them. The rest of his hair he had tied back using long grass weaved together.

"I'm thinking son, that come the morning you need to show me exactly where she is. First light," he responded.

"First light father," the boy said.

He nodded, "Now go help your mother with the little ones. They were causing chaos when I last saw them." His father spoke before sitting back down and continuing to shape the tool he was working on.

At first light, the boy woke his father and they both walked out of the exit of their shelter and stretched, taking in the view around them. Most fires were smoking and some still had embers left inside them.

"Stir the fire quickly then we'll leave," he looked around him, "you really did wake me at first light didn't you?" he said as he noticed the very beginnings of a sunrise over the hills.

"I was waiting till it started to glow," he replied as he watched his father walk over to the bushes behind the shelter.

He returned adjusting his clothing and placing his cloak over his shoulders. "Let's go," he said, "lead the way."

Slowly, the boy retraced his steps looking for the pointers along the way that told him he was going in the right direction. A branch that looked like an arm, a bundle of berry bushes surrounded by oak saplings. Finally, they arrived at the bush he had viewed her from last night and there she was, still sleeping and her fire still burning. She must have woken in the night to add fuel to her fire – she knew how important it was to keep it alive.

"There she is," the boy pointed, ducking behind the bush. However, his father stayed standing and surveyed the child, waiting a few moments as he watched to ensure she was alone. The last thing he needed was to intrude on a matter involving another tribe. It wasn't unknown for tribes to start wars with each other to gain prestige or power or to take resources already claimed by others.

"What are you going to do?" he whispered.

"See where she came from," his father said as he walked around the bush and towards the girl. The crunch of his feet on the ground woke her immediately and she sat bolt upright before backing herself against the entrance of the cave.

"Hush, hush, we won't hurt you," the father said softly reaching out his hand.

Backing away further, she began to mumble incoherently and put her hands up in defence.

"What is she saying?" the boy asked.

"I can't tell, it doesn't sound like us," his father replied. Backing up slightly, he put his hands out to his side, palms facing up in a gesture of peace. "Friend," he said before holding his hand out to her, "friend."

She looked at him and this time he noticed how filthy she was. It wasn't just normal child dirt, her hair was matted with mud and she had grazes and cuts all over her face and arms. For a moment her eyes gazed across him and then took in the child behind. At this, she visibly relaxed and the father beckoned his child closer.

"Come here, son," he said, "your presence is reassuring her."

The boy moved slowly with his hands held out, replicating the gesture of his father and crouched down next to the girl who didn't move away from him.

"Iwot," he said beating his fist against his chest. "I am Iwot," he repeated pointing to himself with two fingers. "You?" he questioned as he used the same two fingers to point at her.

Understanding spread across her face and she almost smiled, "Anika," she responded with a fist against her chest.

Four

Excitement was the emotion she was met with as word spread around the camp of a child found stranded in the woods. Many came out to look at her, stopping their daily tasks to gawp at the stranger who spoke a curious tongue. Iwot's mother came out of the shelter, baby attached to her hip and looked at the child her partner had brought her.

"What have you for me now?" she asked, "there's me thinking you have gone off early to hunt for breakfast and you return with another one of these," she said, gesturing towards the band of children sat around the fire, one of which was rolling pieces of what looked like clay into little balls and making a row of them neatly next to his toes.

"Alone in the woods, no one around. Says her name is Anika," Father replied.

"I thought she didn't speak our tongue," the mother queried.

"No, she doesn't seem to but Iwot got her to understand he was sharing his name," he tousled his son's shaggy brown hair.

Mother took her in, noticing the lack of clothing and cuts and grazes across her face. She also observed a bloodstain on her right side and putting her baby down in the lap of one of her other children, she walked towards the girl. Carefully, she took the girl's head in her hands and moved her face from side to side before gesturing at her to raise her arms. The girl obeyed and cringed as the mother lifted her tunic and prodded at the graze on her side.

"She has packed this well, stopped the infection," Mother said to no one in particular, "she hasn't been alone long, she is too well fed." Taking the girl by the hand, she led her around the fire and into the shelter where they would be out of prying eyes. The father followed her in, with Iwot not far behind him.

"Stay outside please Iwot, the children need you," Mother said.

"But Mother, I found her and…" her glance told him what would happen if he disobeyed so he begrudgingly left the adults alone with the young girl who had sat down on the animal skins around the edges.

"What do you think?" Father asked as he watched his partner busy herself gathering breakfast. She crouched low next to the girl and handed her a cup of water held in a wooden cup carved from the branch of a tree. This was followed by a bowl full of hazelnuts, walnuts and berries which she took with a nod of her head and began to eat swiftly.

"Maybe she was somehow affected by the ground shake. The land around here is softer than normal which suggests a wider flow of water. Strange things have happened in the last few days and now we find her in the woods, alone. It makes sense that she was a part of it." Mother spoke quietly so as not to frighten the child. Her wisdom still astounded him at times and it made him even more thankful that she had been the one chosen for him to raise his family with.

"How can we communicate with her?" Father asked.

Mother shrugged and looked towards the entrance as she heard her youngest begin to whimper. "It's close to feeding time for him. Let's see what we can get from her," she said turning her back to the doorway and crouching low next to Anika.

Father joined her on the floor which was swept clear and was now just a surface of fine earth and minuscule stones.

"Hello," she said to the girl and began to stroke her hair, picking out bits that were stuck there. "Dirty," she said pointing to her hair and her body. "I am San." She said using the same fist gesture as Iwot. "This is Grenn," she continued whilst pointing with two fingers towards Father.

With startling blue eyes, the girl looked up. San thought her hair was blonde underneath all the mud but it was difficult to tell.

"Anika," she said looking directly at San.

"Anika, a beautiful name," replied San.

Starting to mumble again, it was clear Anika wanted to communicate but her language was somewhat different to theirs and she soon accepted that they couldn't understand her.

San started small, pointing to the bowl she said, "bowl."

Anika looked at her, eyes full of tears as she began to contemplate all that had happened to her in the last few days.

"Bowl," San tried again.

Anika caught on, "browl," she responded.

"Almost," San replied, taking the bowl from the floor and holding it towards her, "b ow l" she said, slower this time and pronouncing each sound.

"b ow l, bowl," Anika almost shouted when she thought she had it right.

Grenn laughed, "she is a fast learner."

Suddenly a shadow stood in the doorway and Iwot walked in with the baby in his arms. It was flailing about – kicking its arms and legs in protest at being kept waiting.

"Mother," Iwot pleaded.

"I'm coming," she said, taking the baby from his arms and immediately and skilfully attaching it ready for his breakfast. "Iwot, spend the day with Anika. Take her to do your jobs with you. Talk to her, show her the words for everything." She thought for a moment. "Can we take in another mouth to feed?" she asked Grenn, though they both knew the question was completely rhetorical as neither of them would turn a child away to be attacked by wolves or eaten by a lion.

"Always," Grenn said while placing a loving hand on his son who was busy slurping away at the breakfast his mother provided him. They smiled at each other then left the tent leaving Iwot alone with Anika who was staring at him, her big blue eyes full of expectation and curiosity.

"Come on then," he said. And when she didn't move, "Up, get up, let's go." He gestured for her to follow him and she did, understanding that he wanted her to go with him.

"It's going to be a long day," he said, more to himself than her.

"Day," she replied.

"No, it is going to be a long day," he responded, speaking each word slowly as if this would help her to understand.

"Long day," she said aiming to please him.

"Yes, ok. Well done," he replied rolling his eyes as he walked over to the group of children his age, waiting for him to lead them into the woods to collect firewood for the day's cooking.

Grenn watched from his circle of men who were preparing for their hunt. Many had been working on new weapons crafted from flint mainly and he viewed with pride the work of the men around him. All had spears that had a sharp flint point attached with sinew and a few were sporting bows and arrows made from flexible trees. These were excellent at taking an animal down from further away and helped the men with spears get closer by injuring the animal first. Each man had painted his face with the clay found in this area, this helped to camouflage them and allowed for stealthier tracking of the great beasts. His son was at an age where he would begin to be taken on hunts very soon but for now, his task was to find out where this stranger had come from and if by any chance they would be able to help her home.

Five

It was many months before Anika started talking to them. Understanding came first and she would nod or shake her head and follow directions from all the members of the tribe. With her beautiful blond hair and a contagious smile, she was well-liked by all and had made many friends amongst the children. In the little time they had where they weren't helping prepare food, collecting firewood, making or repairing clothes and other items, Anika enjoyed playing games that the children made up and she was very good at winning those games.

It was coming to the end of summer when she finally starting speaking. The temperature had begun to cool, not rapidly but the sun didn't feel so scorching anymore and there was more rain coming in from the hills. People were having to walk further afield to forage for berries and other fruits. They had almost used up all the Cattail in the area – using the rhizomes at the bottom of the plant as a source of carbohydrate and protein. Anika loved it best when they were cooked on the embers of a fire and then broken open so you could suck the starch from right inside. She loved the sweetness of them and the way the tribe would sit around the fire and eat them together.

While walking back to the camp from the river where they had been digging up those delicious Cattails, she had stopped suddenly and turned towards Iwot who was rambling on about the magic he had seen performed by a wise man at a tribe gathering.

"What is it?" he asked frustrated at her for interrupting his flow of talk. He was just getting to the good bit where the magician had made the bowl of seeds smoke, bang and pop.

"Will we go soon?" she asked.

For a minute, Iwot just stared at her, shocked at the sound of her voice. Having only heard her laugh and cry, hearing her speak was a wonderful sound. "Wow!" he said, his mouth still wide open in disbelief.

"What is wow?" she asked.

"Wow, means amazing, shocking, good, great. You are talking! How long have you been able to talk?" he questioned, excited now at the thought of being able to have an actual conversation with her.

She thought for a moment, moving the Cattail bundle from arm to arm. "Will we go soon?" she repeated the question.

"Go where?" Iwot asked confused by the question.

"Leave the woods, move on," she replied.

"Yes, of course, we will. You know we can't stay in the same place for too long," he replied, looking at her and trying to read the emotion on her face.

"Which way?" she asked.

Iwot thought for a moment and Anika observed how much he looked like his father when he did this. "Back to the coast, I suppose. Winter is easier near the great waters where the fish still live, though we may head closer to the lakes as there is good shelter in caves around there. It will be up to the community, they decide," he said in a very matter of fact way.

"I understand," she said and continued to walk on, setting quite a march until they entered the valley their camp was in. After which, she placed the Cattails down next to the women preparing the food and headed off up the hill to a crag of rocks she liked to sit on when she needed time alone.

Iwot added his bundle of Cattail to the pile and proceeded towards his tent in the hope of retrieving his drinking cup as the walk had made him thirsty. Before he got there, however. his mother had blocked his way.

"Iwot, what have you done to Anika this time?" she asked with an accusation. She stood tall with her hands on her hips and for once no baby attached. Women of this time tended to keep their very young close at hand due to wild animals. Only last summer, one of the ladies in the tribe had lost her small baby to a wolf who snatched it from outside her tent. The mother was only two metres away but was no match for a wolf running at full speed.

"What Mother? Honestly, it wasn't me this time," he replied slightly aggrieved by his mother's suggestion that Anika's moods were caused by him.

Removing her hands from her hips, San gazed towards the rocks where Anika sat arms folded around her knees looking towards the great water far from where they were. "What is it then? What has happened?" she asked concern filling her voice.

"I'm not sure. She asked me if we are leaving here soon," he said nonchalantly.

"What? Did she ask you? You mean she spoke to you? With words?" his mother sounded overly excited by this fact.

"Yes mother, what else do people speak with?" he responded teasing her now as he knew how much it meant to his mother that she had finally decided to communicate.

Finally, she caught on to his teasing. He had always been the one who enjoyed a joke the most, the one child of her six living children who longed to watch the magicians at tribal gatherings. "Iwot, enough now. What happened?"

He laughed, enjoying his mother's smiles and the little moments he got to spend with her.

"I'm not sure, I don't really understand how girls think. But one minute she was asking me about where we intend to spend the winter and the next she was all silent and moody and then she marched off up the hill," he motioned towards where Anika was sat, still in the same position. "I don't know what's wrong with her."

"Ok, Iwot, thank you. I'll speak to her," she ruffled his hair then as an afterthought turned back around.

"Can you please get your brothers and sisters from Madchen she is watching them over by her shelter?"

"Ok," he said feeling the burden of being the oldest in the family. He'd had an older brother once – he was eleven collections of seasons in fact, but he had died in a climbing accident and they no longer spoke of him. It was believed by his tribe that if they spoke of the dead the higher forces would think that they were ungrateful for their lives and would take them to the spirit world also. Because of this, once a member of the tribe was dead it was as if they had never been alive in the first place.

Watching as his mother walked off towards Anika, he forgot about his need for water and walked in the direction of his siblings. He could hear their screams before he even got there but the welcome he got from them was always worth the stress of supervising them.

Anika could see someone approaching her from the corner of her eye. Even when her thoughts were elsewhere, she had been trained by her father to always be observant of what was around her – it could save her life.

"Hello Anika, may I join you?" San asked not wanting to disturb the child's thoughts.

"Yes," she said and shuffled up on her rock to make space for San.

"Iwot told me you were talking. What brought that on?" she asked curious about the child and wanting to find out exactly what had happened to her all those months ago.

"I noticed that resources were running low and I know this means we will go soon," she replied hesitantly revealing her true thoughts.

"You are right. The community will meet tonight to discuss where we will be heading. Winter can be brutal here and we need to ensure we have sufficient shelter and resources for the time," San said.

"Brutal?" Anika questioned, even now still hearing words she didn't understand.

San smiled, "It means hard, tough, not easy on the people," she gestured towards the group below, always busily going about necessary tasks to keep them alive. San viewed Iwot down by the big fire pit entertaining the youngsters with a trick using sticks and small mud balls. He had them all laughing as usual.

Anika nodded her head, "I understand."

San observed the girl – she was turning more beautiful daily and would be a wonderful match for one of the younger boys one day. And at that, it hit her, why she seemed so sad today. Would she still be here? When she reached an age where she proved her worthiness to the tribe – would she leave and search for her people?

She took her hand, "Anika, are you worried about moving further from your father? Your people?"

Tears began to fall down her cheeks and she nodded, looking up into San's eyes and biting her lip to stop herself from crying.

"It would be hard to find them any way you know. People don't stay still for long. Do you even know the name of your tribe or the area they were in?" San asked thinking it unlikely.

Surprisingly, Anika responded with a nod, "yes, they were the tribe of the frozen forest," she smiled at memories flooding her mind. "We moved south to find better weather and to follow rumours we had heard of vast lands with plentiful resources. My father told me that his father had met other tribes on the way that couldn't believe there were still people living in the north because of the ice of course. Because of this, they named us the frozen forest tribe. We didn't know tribes were meant to have names but they all seemed to or all the ones we met anyway. So we kept it."

"There is always a story behind a tribe's name," San commented.

“I have never asked yours,” Anika said.

“You have never asked much,” she laughed, “our tribe has been around for thousands of years they say. It is one of the oldest. We started way to the East and travelled many thousands of years across plains, plateaus and mountain passes. Throughout all this time, our tribe was followed or watched over by a golden eagle – its wings were said to be the largest ever seen and its eyes bulged. Stories said that he had one eye on us and one eye on our way forward,” she smiled and looked out across her people beginning to join together in the central circle to prepare their evening meal.

“Once we arrived in this land it left us but occasionally it is spotted, perched high overlooking our tribe and ensuring its safety. Of course, we haven’t been without loss,” as she thought of her lost children, “but we have never starved or been unable to find resources for our people, unlike other tribes. I like to think it’s always here watching us from afar.” For a moment, she stared off into the distance and Anika followed her gaze hoping to see this great flying bird that San spoke about with such conviction on her face.

“Anyway,” she began again, “that is why we are called the tribe of the Golden Eagle,” she finished, then stood up holding her hand out to Anika, the girl took her hand and together they began to walk back towards the camp. As they approached, San stopped and turning to Anika she said, "ne day, you may search for your father and you may find him but until that day and even after it you will always be considered a member of the tribe of the Golden Eagle. Don't forget that."

"I won't," responded Anika and the sound of her voice once again made San smile as they had waited so long to hear it.

Six

The hunting group didn't return that evening. No one seemed overly concerned as it wasn't unusual for a hunting group to stray farther afield than intended and then find the sun lower than expected after the hunt was complete. They made do with Cattail pancakes – made after grinding the roots using stones to produce flour, an array of wild vegetables such as carrot and parsnip and Ransoms (wild garlic), mint and thyme to add flavour. There were a few small birds removed of their feathers and roasted that Iwot and some of the other boys had managed to kill with slingshots. After this, they ate berries, small apples and a range of nuts. Even without the meat, all were full by the time they left the fire pit and headed to their shelters.

Before heading to her furs to lie down for the night, Anika walked towards the flowing stream where they collected their water. Using San's water container – an Ostrich egg with the top chopped off, egg drained from the inside and cleaned out – she collected enough water for the night. San got particularly thirsty when she was nursing the baby. As she walked back, she saw shadows further down the stream and recognised the voices of San and Affeyso who was the tribe's Wiseman. As she approached she took in how Affeyso stood. He was an old man, ancient some said, no one knew how many seasons he had seen pass, but some of his stories suggested he had been a part of the tribe who crossed the continent with the protection of the Golden Eagle. Though how this was possible no one knew. Some who were unsure whether his tales were true only had to look at his appearance to convince themselves. Reaching almost to his toes when unplaited was a long white beard that began at his nose and worked its self across his face and down his chin only leaving space where his mouth was. His eyebrows were wild – curly white hairs sprouted from just above his eyes, which some said were long enough to be plaited also. His eyes were very similar to Anika's in colour – a startling blue that almost looked like a pool of water if it weren't for the black dot in the middle. He wore the clothing of an important person – his cloak was made of the fur of a polar bear (something most of them had never seen), and unusually his tunic underneath had the hood of a cave lion with the head, eyes, teeth, ears all still intact. Younger children in the tribe were scared of it and stayed away from the wise man for fear the lion was still alive. Although wise, he was a fun-loving man who enjoyed teasing the little ones with the hood and laughing as they ran off with little screams. All of this fascinated Anika but most of all it was his treasures that intrigued her the most. Around his neck, he wore a necklace of intricate shapes that were all carved from the bones of animals. The detail on them was unbelievable. As well as this, his cloak had rows of delicate shells threaded into the fur that contrasted against the white and made the whole cloak a work of wonder and a talking piece amongst the children who created stories about where he could have got such a beautiful ensemble.

However, it wasn't this that caught her today but the conversation they were having. She stood in plain sight to them but they didn't stop their talk. Nothing was hidden even from the littlest members of the tribe. Life was tough and they were taught to deal with it from very early on.

"I do not like the look of the stars tonight San," he said twisting a part of his beard around his finger and leaning on the stick he now used to help him walk.

"What is it that concerns you?" San replied, looking at the sky, which to Anika looked the same as any other night. In a time before pollution and artificial lighting, the stars were so bright and clear they could be viewed even through the clouds. Tonight, however, there were no clouds and the sky was full to bursting with dazzling stars that competed against the brightness of a full moon.

"There are some missing," he said, "like their life has been extinguished. I have seen it before when stars disappear never to return." He looked down at his feet, bare at the moment as he disliked wearing shoes when the weather was warm. "I fear it is a sign."

Gazing into the serious eyes of the man she considered to be her father, San bit her lip before responding. Anika knew this as a sign she was worried. On the first night she had arrived, she saw her do it. When Toa, her second youngest, had caught a fever and it had taken days to break and when Anika had returned to the camp without Iwot after disagreeing. At all these times she had seen San bite her bottom lip.

"The men?" she questioned.

"It is a possibility San," he replied, "not one we ever wish to consider but preparation is key." He began to walk away from her. "We must prepare."

San didn't follow him immediately, she walked towards Anika and, putting her arm around her shoulders, she gave a big sigh. "I'm going to need your help," she said walking back towards the camp.

That night dragged on and on. The women of the camp had put their younger children to bed then followed the instructions of Affeyso and the medicine women. When they were all ready, San insisted that they all tried to sleep but as Anika lay there, she could see that she wasn't the only one in the tent who was wide awake. San was lying between Toa and the baby (they didn't name children until their 8th season as so many died before they reached that point), and Iwot was rolling back and forth on the mat next to his brothers trying to get comfortable.

Anika looked out through the hole in the top of the tent and saw the stars still twinkling as if they had no idea the turmoil they were causing.

"Anika, you must try to sleep," San whispered over the heads of her children.

"I know," she replied and she rolled over with her face to the sides of the animal skins stretched between branches. Slowly, she drifted off but her dreams were full and her sleep was disturbed.

Seven

It wasn't until late the following afternoon that next day that the hunting party returned. Dati and Tolli (Iwot's younger brothers) were on watch on the tops of the hills facing the valley the men had walked through early yesterday morning. The boys were chewing on dandelion roots when they saw the first men walk around the corner of the craggy rocks set to the side of the valley. It was clear there was something wrong as some of the men were being supported by others as they limped along and one was being carried in a stretcher hastily put together with branches and reeds. Dati stood up and howled at the top of his voice – his wild call is what they called it – it gained the attention of the tribe below who began to run towards the path the men were approaching from.

"Dati, look," his brother Tolli called, pointing towards the group of men.

Tolli followed his brother's pointed finger and saw his father carrying hunks of meat on his back. There were cuts and grazes all over his arms and legs and a huge cut on his forehead that must have bled considerably as there was dry blood down his cheek but he was walking.

"Come on," Dati shouted, grabbing his brother's arm and running down the hill through the tall grass back to the camp.

As he approached the camp, Iwot ran towards him. "Get water now, lots and lots. Keep bringing it – don't stop until we tell you to." And with that, he ran back towards the camp.

Quickly, the boys did as instructed, thankful for a task to keep them occupied.

The men kept arriving in small groups, each one carrying a slab of meat from whatever animal they had hunted. Around the fire pit, people were bustling, each one aware of their task at hand. A collection of Plantain leaves had been put in a basket to the side last night and these were being used now as sturdy bandages for the multitude of cuts and grazes that the men had received. Looking closely, Iwot watched as the women cleaned the men's wounds with Sphagnum moss soaked in water from the river. Its absorbent qualities were tremendous and they used it frequently – picking and storing it whenever they could. Surprise filled everyone's faces with a man called Flur, who was at present unconscious lying on an animal fur next to the fire, his wound revealed what looked like claw marks from his armpit to his belly. Whispers broke out from the crowd.

"Is that the mark of the lion?"

"How can it be?"

"They are far from here?"

Suddenly, Affeyso appeared from behind the cluster of women surrounding Flur. "Enough!" he shouted, "let us not become distracted. Questions can be answered when the time is right."

Immediately the women obeyed and begun again to treat the wounded. Medicine women produced their wares of dried herbs and began distributing as needed. Many of the herbs could be used by anyone as their uses were well known and it was difficult to go wrong with them. However, one plant was kept apart from the rest as if given incorrectly or in too high a dose it could prove fatal. That day it was given to three men.

Anika helped all she could, remembering the skills her father had taught her. Cleansing wounds, packing with clay to prevent infection, bandaging if needed, but she noticed the medicine women mashing up and feeding the worst wounded of the men a concoction of dark berries and dry leaves. When the moment seemed right, she asked San what they were.

"It's Belladonna. It can be poisonous if too much is ingested so only the experienced medicine women can use it," she answered.

"What does it do?" she asked as she watched one man barely conscious painfully swallow a dose.

"It dulls the pain," she said before heading off to help others.

Anika watched as the man slowly closed his eyes and looked as if he was barely breathing.

"Leave him be, Anika," Taip said gently, "he will join the spirit world soon."

Understanding that this meant that soon he would die, Anika turned. Soon his family joined him and held him, crying silently as he slipped away.

Later that evening, when the chaos had subsided, Anika slipped into the tent where she sat down on her skin.

For a moment, she stroked the hair on the mat beside her – it was coarser now, having been off the animal for some time. As she did, tears streamed down her face and she took her hand off the mat and hugged her legs. Quickly, her muffled cries turned into sobs. A moment later, Grenn walked in. Exhausted from the hunt and all the events that had occurred alongside it, he had wanted to take some time to rest whilst the women began preparing the meat – life carried on quickly for them.

"Anika, what is it, child? What is wrong?" Grenn sat down beside her and put his arm around her. She buried her head in his chest and continued to cry. After a while, her sobs subsided and Grenn lifted her chin so she would look at him. "What is wrong?" he knew it couldn't be what she had witnessed outside as accidents occurred regularly in their world and blood and death weren't new to her.

She shook her head not thinking he would understand her.

"You can tell me anything Anika. We are family," he said.

"I miss him," she said through her whimpers.

"Your father?" he asked.

Nodding her head, she looked up at him and watched his face as he scratched his beard and thought for a moment.

"You need to be careful talking about him," he said reluctantly.

"Why?" she asked.

"Because if we speak of the dead we are ungrateful to still be living," he said.

Suddenly, Anika jumped up and shouted at him angrily. "My father is not dead!"

"Maybe not," he conceded, "but it is best not to speak of him."

Turning around with her back to him she thought for a moment before coming to a decision. "I don't believe that," she said quietly.

"Anika, we shouldn't," he responded.

She turned towards him, "I don't believe it."

Before continuing to speak, she crouched down in front of him, "In my tribe, we mourn our dead. We have a special ceremony for them and everybody speaks about them: then, now, forever. We never forget them and we know we will see them again when we join them in the spirit world whenever our time comes," she stopped talking and put her hands on his face. "You will not die just because you speak about the ones you loved."

Grenn shook his head, "I can't, Anika."

She stood up, "then I am saddened for you. But don't ever tell me again not to talk about my father. I will not forget him." With that, she pulled back the flaps of the door and left.

Eight

That evening, the community met around the fire after dinner. Every member of the tribe was there apart from the small children who were being watched in one of the tents. Affeyso sat on the large stone to which other smaller stones and logs were connected, it formed a circle around the fire which was burning brightly, lighting up all the faces of the people sat around it.

"As you may be aware, we have a problem," he began, "when our men were hunting Wildebeest just beyond the valley, they were set upon by a pride of Cave Lions. Not one, but multitudes. It is unusual for this type of animal to attack without provocation. There were no young to protect and they hadn't been disturbed. It was a deliberate, unprovoked attack – almost like a band of Coyotes. As you know we lost six men – four of them were fathers. Their children will need to be taken under the care of the tribe and their sons taught by the other men of the tribe as is our custom." He paused briefly looking around the circle at the nodding heads, he knew from this that they would arrange this amongst themselves. The tribe always looked after its own. He continued, "this brings us back to the Cave Lions and the question as to why they attacked?" He stopped talking and sat back, which meant the others could begin to comment.

"Maybe they were after the meat." Lonn, a tall man who was a master with a bow and arrow, suggested.

"If so, why did they leave it behind after the attack?" Grenn said.

"Is it possible that you scared them off?" San asked.

"Unlikely, only when we began to wade into the river did they retreat. The meat was right there – we had begun to carve it up. It was ripe for the taking," answered Grenn.

"Why would they attack so sporadically?" Sonq asked.

"And so viciously," added Gilda, who had lost her partner in the attack. San placed her hand on Gildas. Comfort for those who lost loved ones was only allowed up to the point of their burial which would take place tomorrow.

"It is concerning," Grenn said.

The circle went quiet for a brief moment until Stol spoke up. She too had lost her partner today, they had four children together, one of which had been born only weeks before. That baby was in her arms now – fast asleep, oblivious to the devastation that had taken place earlier in the day. Anika observed her. Of all the women in the tribe she admired Stol the most. She wore her hair in plaits as many of the women did but hers always looked so tidy. They curled up around the sides of her head and allowed the escape of short curly blonde locks to frame her face. But the thing Anika admired the most was her skill with weapons. Out of all the women in the tribe, she was the only one that took part in hunting expeditions or so Anika was told. When she had arrived, many months before, Stol had been far gone in her pregnancy but she did still practise with a slingshot and bow and arrow and Anika had seen her harpoon fish in the river with skill and ease. She longed to learn her skills but what she said next irritated Anika and brought up feelings she had already shared with Grenn.

"Maybe the higher forces are punishing us," she spoke solemnly with a catch in her throat, all her strength at present sapped by her grief.

The group began to mumble and murmur, discussing seriously the suggestion made by Stol. Affeyso listened to each point raised and nodded his head in agreement, Anika could stand it no longer.

"It has nothing to do with Higher forces!" she yelled, shouting over the whole circle and forcing it to quieten. At that point, the slight breeze that had provided refreshment throughout the day picked up and could be heard twisting through the trees. Almost making them sound like they were laughing at her and her suggestion.

Affeyso ignored the wind and looked directly at her. "What do you mean child?" he asked, deliberately using the word 'child' to remind her of her status.

"I just think that things happen for a reason and it is neither a punishment or reward from Higher forces," she sighed, unsure whether she should have spoken up or not.

"Where I came from we spoke about Higher forces with joy and happiness, believing that they were there to help us and encourage us and leading a good life would please them." Many were nodding in agreement at this. "However…" she started, pausing before carrying on as her courage began to leave her, "we never believed they would punish us if we didn't live well or send things that would hurt us. Life is hard and sometimes horrible things happen. We have to move on because out here you wouldn't survive if you didn't." She stopped and looked directly at Grenn who was staring at her with a mixture of disbelief and pride in his eyes, "I don't believe that higher forces would want us to forget the people we loved or swallow our grief or else face the spirit world. We have brains far greater than our ancestors and they have been given to us so we use them wisely. All this talk of being punished by something we cannot see is just foolish." And at that, she finished. Unfortunately, her words were not taken well by the majority of the camp who began to argue and shout. Shifting back on the log she was sat on, she wanted to shrink so no one could see her. Suddenly, she felt Grenn's hand on her own and this renewed her courage.

Affeyso quietened the crowd by lifting his hand. "We thank you for your brave comments young lady and appreciate that your tribe may have believed differently. But as you well know we are the tribe of the Golden Eagle which was sent by higher powers. If we live our lives the way that is expected of us then protection will come forth.

If for some reason we have slipped from our path then a sacrifice will need to be made to please the spirit world." At this, he rose from his spot and began to walk away. This was a sign that the meeting was at an end. The crowd dispersed hurriedly, all wanting to be with their loved ones for fear of the Cave Lions reappearing.

As Anika walked back to her tent, no one spoke to her. Just as she was about to enter Affeyso was at her side. "A word, Anika," he said, not unkindly but she was daunted by the idea of speaking alone with this wise man. They walked to the outskirts of the camp and stopped at the river, lazily twisting and turning away. He turned to face her, his face looked even older in the moonlight this evening and she could see how events, such as this, took their toll on him as everyone looked to him for answers.

"Sometimes," he began, "people need to be controlled. Without control, mayhem and chaos occur. If people are allowed to think their own thoughts it would be like setting a fire without clearing the ground first. Something that can be so useful, people, will become a destructive force that only bad will come from." He looked at her and held her hand, "do you understand that?" he asked.

She took a moment to think about it, staring out at the trickling stream in front of her.

"I think so. You allow people to believe in something that might not be true to make sure they all behave in the way you want them to," she rephrased his words.

"Not the way I want them to, but the way they *need* to keep them alive," he said.

"But *my* tribe don't believe this and they are still alive," she said, almost in a whisper, not sure whether she wanted him to hear her or not, but she was unable to stop the words from coming out of her mouth.

"Your tribe have a different story. Here, this works and whether you like it or not it is the way it is. We cannot spend weeks, months or years thinking about those we have lost. If we don't move on quickly from our troubles then we may as well be dead, because the perilous world we live in won't wait for your grief to subside," he replied.

"I see," was all she could think of in response though deep inside she wasn't convinced by his words.

Looking at her, he could see this was the case and her wisdom for one of such a young age astounded him.

"So, can I rely on you to not talk about this with the tribe again?" he questioned, his voice forceful and leaving her little choice.

For a moment, she waited. This tribe were, at present, her family and, until she was of an age where she had the skill to be on her own, she had no choice but to be a part of them. "Yes," she said quietly.

"Thank you," he said before dropping her hand and walking her back to her tent, "sleep well," he commanded before walking away towards his shelter.

Nine

As the weather became cooler and the leaves began to turn, the tribe's thoughts turned to preparation for the coming winter. Sometimes they were long and always hazardous. The majestic beauty of the forest could be seen in all its wonder from the tops of the hills. The trees created a cascading palette of reds, oranges and yellows that rippled like waves as the breeze caught them.

"Anika," San called from the front of the foraging party. Due to the approaching winter, the foragers were busier than normal. Stores of berries, nuts and fungi were needed and it was their job to ensure they were plentiful.

"Yes?" Anika replied, holding the hand of Kaie who had a face covered with berries.

San looked at her and smiled, "I think Kaie is eating more than she is picking."

Looking down at the child, she could see San was right.

San continued, "Can you and Iwot head over to the Oak trees and gather branches, leaves and acorn? The medicine women will need them. Take Dati and Tolli with you."

"What do they use them for?" Anika asked, interested in all things to do with treating illnesses.

San continued to pick blackberries from the flourishing bushes as she responded to Anika's questions, "I think they are used to treat pains in the stomach, soreness and I'm not sure what else. And we ground the acorns for flour as well," she looked at Anika and smiled, "now off you go."

Turning around the way they had come, Anika followed a well-trod path through the forest until they came to the trees greatly recognisable by their lobed leaves with rounded edges. Iwot walked ahead as he considered himself to be the leader of this little group and Anika ensured the two younger boys were keeping up. Throughout the rest of the afternoon, they collected. Each one filling their woven baskets full to the brim.

"It's time to be getting back.," Iwot said, viewing the sky through the trees and recognising its darkening.

“You’re right, boys let’s go.,” Anika agreed.

Despite their heavy loads, they made good speed and were in sight of the camp from the top of the hill in no time. Suddenly, from behind them, they heard a low growl. All four of them froze, immediately identifying the sound. Only Iwot dared to peek behind him and what he saw sent shivers running down his spine and sweat forming at his temples. Snaking out from behind the bushes was a Cave Lion, its hind legs stretched out as if it had just been disturbed from its slumber. It flexed its claws and yawned, revealing its long sharp teeth.

“Don’t move,” Iwot whispered, “now slowly turn sideways to face it.”

Without hesitation, all three children obeyed. Fear, they knew, was something that could get them killed, they had to face it.

“When I start, you need to follow. As loud as you can, make yourself look as large as you can. As you do so, back away slowly but don’t turn your back to it,” Iwot spoke quickly and with conviction. “Now!” he shouted.

At that, all children began to roar, screeching and screaming with their arms out wide while very slowly retreating backwards. The lion watched. Pacing back and forth, it growled and scraped its feet in the ground, but didn't come forward. Continuing to shout and yell as loudly as possible, the children had put some space between themselves and the Cave Lion. The commotion they made alerted the camp and out of the corner of her eye, Anika could see the men slowly approaching the hill below them with weapons in their hands. Next to them, came the rest of the tribe who were also replicating the movements the children were making. Watching closely, the lion took a few steps forwards as it was unable to see the children now they had gone over the ridge of the hill. Grenn and the other men were now at the sides of the children and they enclosed around them protecting them from the lion above. San reached her boys and grabbed them quickly before retreating down the hill. Iwot pulled Anika by the hand and raced to the camp where they stood around the fire, adding branches to make it larger in the knowledge that lions won't approach the fierce flames. From this point, they watched the men meet the fearsome lion at the top of the hill. The noise they made was far louder than the one the children made as they waved their weapons in the air. None of the men attacked the lion as a fight was not what they wanted. Having already witnessed the devastating injuries a lion could cause once this summer, it wasn't something they desired. Slowly, the lion retreated, back into the forest and away from the camp. Two men were left to tail it, to ensure it moved far enough away from the camp.

When he returned, Grenn sought out Affeyso and a discussion began. One by one, the community joined them until a decision could be reached. Anika chose to sit with the younger children this time as she didn't want to be involved in the talks tonight. Her thoughts kept turning back to the lion. In her short life, she had never been that close to one before and she felt shaky just thinking about it. Dati and Tolli however couldn't stop sharing their ordeal with the younger children and it made her smile to hear them tell their tale over and again.

It was late by the time the adults returned and the children had helped themselves to the boar meat which had been roasting on a spit over the fire. They were just beginning to supplement it with dandelion leaves and buttercups when they noticed Affeyso return to his shelter. San and Gren approached the fire and summoned their children back to the tent, as did the other parents whilst some men stayed up to guard the camp for the evening.

"Iwot, have you filled the water containers for the evening?" Grenn asked.

"Yes," he responded.

San settled the younger children down.

"What is happening?" Iwot asked as he sensed the stress radiating from his parents.

"We leave tomorrow," Grenn replied.

"Is that necessary?" Iwot asked.

San looked at Grenn then answered Iwot, "Unfortunately, yes. For some reason, the Cave Lions have left their usual territory and have wandered further towards our camp. We cannot risk another unprovoked attack like the last one. When our children are in danger, there is no choice."

Anika thought for a minute, "Are we ready?" she asked thinking about the winter looming ahead. Only this morning she had seen a flock of birds in formation heading for the south where the weather was warmer.

If only people could fly, she thought.

"We have no choice Anika," she paused, "that is why we intend to head to the South West.

This took Anika by surprise and for a moment she stood silently before being approached by Grenn.

He spoke, "I know to you this seems like a step away from your family but it is a matter of surviving the winter and our best chance is to head as far south as possible. There is said to be lakes with plentiful fish and reeds that will grow throughout the winter. It is about the survival of the tribe Anika. Can you understand that?"

Nodding her head, she looked up into the eyes of the man who had taken her in and made her one of his own.

"Of course, Grenn," she said.

That night as the camp slept, she dreamt of her father and his voice calling for her when the waters swept her away. Tears flowed down her cheeks, before she finally woke with the morning sun.

Ten

When the tribe awoke that morning, they were determined to set off before the sun reached its highest point. Every person in the tribe, young or old, were given a task to ensure they achieved this goal. The watchmen had returned in the early hours of the morning to confirm that the lion had led them back to its pride which was fifteen strong and held many cubs. They were only two miles away from the camp and, considering a lion can run as fast as fifty miles an hour in short bursts, the camp knew their decision to leave immediately had been the right one. With the pride that close, they were sure to hunt the same animals at some point soon which was a fruitless danger.

Anika noticed that only Affeyso sat seemingly completing no task, but when you looked closely you could see his lips moving and his hands making small gestures.

He was praying to the higher beings for a safe journey for his people. Being from the tribe of the frozen forest, Anika had heard many stories about perilous journeys into unknown territory and many people had been lost from her tribe as they marched further south to escape the last of the ice.

By breakfast time, the camp was in full flow towards preparation – none took the time to stop and eat knowing full well that the sun would eventually give up its fight and slip from the sky once more. Anika and Iwot had been put on water. This meant they had to collect the containers used to carry water and fill each one to the top before returning it to its owner. This was fine when the containers were empty as many had useful straps that rested across their shoulders, but when they were full it made for heavy work. Neither child dared stop, however, as they had already witnessed today many children and even some adults receiving cutting remarks from men in the group who were concerned about their progression towards preparation to depart.

"Will we have enough?" Anika asked Iwot.

"Of course," he said, not looking up from the containers he was busily filling. Once finished, she tied each one with the cord made from plant fibres that had been laboriously woven together and then threaded through holes in the top of the animal skin. Anika had seen excellently made needles that were painstakingly carved pieces of bone and she too had been taught the skill of sewing. It was the large ostrich egg containers that made their lives difficult today, as each one came with a carefully selected pebble that fit the hole made in the top perfectly. Many of the containers had this pebble connected to some cord that wrapped around the egg and acted like a carrying handle. However, on the odd occasion, this wasn't the case and the pebble had become mixed up with the ones sat on the side of the stream, it would take a while for them to work their way through them to ensure they had selected the right one.

"Why don't you keep it in your hand while you are filling the container?" Anika asked as she witnessed Iwot searching through the pebbles close to him for yet another of the stoppers.

Iwot looked at her and scowled, he had trouble admitting when Anika was right and found it irritating that the girl always seemed to have an answer for everything. "This is the way I do it," he said, refusing to even consider her suggestion.

"Do what you want," said Anika shrugging her shoulders and beginning to walk away loaded with a fresh batch of water containers.

"You aren't supposed to walk around without me," Iwot said. The camp community had imposed a rule for the day that everyone had to be a part of at least a pair, which was a precaution taken to ensure safety if the lions should return.

Anika turned back to look at him, still struggling to find the lost pebble amongst the stones. "I can take care of myself," she shrugged and turned away again.

"Fine," he shouted, "go ahead, let a lion eat you. I hear they swallow little girls whole. You'd be living in its belly for years before it decided to digest you."

Anika knew this wasn't true but frowned at the harshness of his words.

"I can kill a lion," she said.

"Oh, sure you can. What with your slingshot?" he asked mocking her now. Anika was known to be excellent with a slingshot but the small stones she used as ammunition would give a lion a headache and make it very angry but nothing more.

"I can learn to hunt," she said matter of fact.

"Girls don't do hunting," Iwot stated.

"Doesn't mean they can't start. I will learn hunting too. I am strong like you and can run faster than you can."

"You'll need to do a lot of running when you miss and they come charging," Iwot laughed, "you could always get on your knees, flutter your eyelids and beg the nasty mammoth not to eat you – that's what girls do." Iwot forgot about his search for the pebble and got down on his knees with his hands in a praying position, "oh please nice Mr Mammoth, please don't hurt me."

At this Anika's rage came forth. She took her slingshot from her waist, picked up a small stone and loosed it straight at Iwot. It got him right below his eye on his cheekbone. He collapsed to the ground, clutching his cheek and howling.

"Owwww!" he said loudly.

Anika ran to him, her annoyance forgotten in an instant, but quickly returned when she saw his face once again teasing her.

"Oh no please, little girl – don't hurt me anymore," Iwot chuckled, though his eyes were full of tears and his face showed pain.

Anika was satisfied that her shot had resulted in proving her point and even more so when she saw the giant bruise begin to appear on the top of his cheekbone right below his eye. Every now and then he would touch it and flinch.

See, she thought, *I am strong.*

When they returned to the camp, Grenn and San noticed the bruise on Iwot's face but didn't ask what had happened. It wasn't the first time Iwot had received an injury from Anika and it wouldn't be the last. Sometimes the boy went too far with his teasing and he needed someone to set him straight. Their oldest son, Rhun, had been the one to do that many years before but since his death, there had been no one until Anika. Both parents dwelled on that thought of their son. San only for a brief moment then she moved on as commanded to do so, so she believed, by the spirit world. However, Grenn held the thought, remembering his oldest and how he would spend hours teaching Iwot how to carve a weapon or tie a cord. He was a kind boy and would have made an exceptional father. His fleeting thoughts brought a smile to his face and San watched him closely, concerned that he had continued the thoughts she had so rapidly extinguished. Only when Iwot approached them did he snap out of his daze and instructed him to make a Sphagnum press for his swiftly growing bruise.

Just before the sun began to wind its way slowly down, the tribe were ready. They ate before they left fuelling the long walk ahead of them. Hunters had been out this morning and had brought back deer which had been cooking for most of the morning. When all had feasted and the last embers of the fire had been wiped out, they set off. Grenn and Lonn were at the front leading the way, whilst the women with young children were encased in the middle for protection. Affeyso carried the ember which would light their next fire wherever they were. He did this between two shells carefully selected from the coast. This allowed enough protection from wind and enough oxygen to ensure it could still breathe. It was a lot quicker and easier to start a fire this way than to begin the lengthy process of starting one with sparking flint stones or friction of wood, especially if they had to stop late at night. Tribes marched for miles in those days, only stopping for occasional comfort breaks and at mealtimes. The Tribe of the Golden Eagle walked swiftly, most in animal fur sandals or shoes whilst some, mainly children, chose to walk in bare feet, something they were used to doing and had hardened their soles considerably.

Luckily, the weather held for them and they started and concluded their journey that day under a warm autumn sun, that dropped below the hills and signalled to them that they needed to start finding a suitable place to camp for the night. As they had filled up their water containers at the last stream they had passed, they decided to camp in a clearing between a set of rolling hills and another forest. Unfortunately, there was no source of water that would allow them fresh water for the morning but also protection from wild animals as not many would venture across. Although as Grenn later pointed out, Cave Lions could swim and if desperate enough would do so.

"Only one night here, we'll need to build enough fires, one per four family groups and sleep in sets with watchmen at corners." Grenn directed the other men, taking on the role of group leader although this wasn't the case. However, because of the experience he had, the men and women in the group accepted his authority quite readily.

All in the tribe busied themselves preparing fires. One first from the still glowing ember Affeyso carried and then the rest were lit when the first fire was raging. Soon the area was glowing with the warmth of almost half a dozen fires which came just in time as the cold autumn evening set in. A dozen or so hunters were sent out – to include Stol and another woman in training – to gather as many hares, squirrels and birds as they could before the light completely left them. Within half an hour, they had returned with over ten hares, a feast of birds and a few squirrels. With the almond flour they had ground throughout the summer, they created a meal of almond flat cakes with meat and roots. Shifts were handed out to guard throughout the night, as they were in unknown territory so needed to be prepared for all dangers lurking.

Anika took her place around her family's fire with Kaie and Tolli snuggled up next to her. After the long journey of the day, within minutes all were asleep.

Rain lashed them from all directions, pouring into their clothing and coating their hair – soaking them within seconds. Anika carried Toa in her back sling and she was shrouded in the animal skins Anika was wearing so most of the rain was off her. Surprisingly, weather like this normally makes the tribe march faster and it would have today had the ground not become a sodden mess. Each footstep was twice as difficult due to the depth to which your foot sunk into the ground. It had been weeks since they began their journey and by the feel of the cold rain on her face, Anika could tell that winter was well and truly on its way. Through the darkness of the day, she thought she could make out silhouettes of hills on the horizon but she wasn't sure. At lunch, they stopped, very briefly exchanging food and water and ensuring everyone had the energy to continue. Anika asked Iwot to check on Toa who was still strapped to her back.

"Fast asleep," reported Iwot.

Anika smiled, this always seemed to be the case when they travelled. "Makes the journey go quicker," she responded.

"For her, anyway," said Iwot passing her a hardened acorn cake that she bit into, then used a swig of water to soften. They also had some hare that had been smoked last night to preserve it for some days and ensure it stayed edible.

"Father says these are the hills we are heading for," he gestured to the silhouettes ahead that Anika had been unsure were even there.

"What is he hoping to find?" Anika asked.

Iwot shrugged, "shelter for the winter I assume. It is coming."

"Does the whiteness fall here?" she asked, interested in the land that wasn't her own but which she was making a home.

"Of course, not all winter but it will come." And with that, they began to march again and, as they drew closer to the hills, Anika began to wonder what they may find there and if it would be what Grenn was hoping for.

Eleven

Finally, the rain let up and the sun popped a curious eye around the clouds to view the work the rain had made for it. With the ceasing of the downpour, came the tribe's glorious first view of the hills ahead of them. They were large, but not so immense that they couldn't be scaled by the entire tribe, and that was exactly what they intended to do. Everyone followed as they were led up the hills and in no time they were stood at the top of one. The sun shone with force, drying the land. All around, the beautiful greenery cascaded like waves as far as the eye could see. One hill after another and cutting straight through the middle was a river – it wasn't big, but enough to find fish and become a plentiful supply of drinking water. Anika thought she could make out another blue expanse, as the hills let up and became flat ground again but she wasn't sure. Looking around her, she saw many of the women taking the opportunity to gather dandelion and buttercups from the hillside which could be used later to supplement their meal.

Suddenly, Dati came running up to her, closely followed by Tolli, he was shouting and waving his hands trying to get attention. Grenn noticed first and beckoned him over.

"What is it, son?" he asked.

Breathing hard from his run up the hill, he struggled for breath and bent over briefly before answering, "Woolly Mammoth, a whole group – down by the river, taking on water it looks like."

"How many?" asked Grenn, as he beckoned his hunters over.

This time Tolli replied, wanting to be involved in the discovery. "About five near this end and a few more further downriver. There is a baby."

It was this part of the discovery that excited the boys more. Baby mammoths were easier to hunt and kill as they weren't used to the threat of humans yet. It wasn't just the meat the tribe wanted. Mammoth, even baby Mammoth, were large enough to provide new clothing for at least ten people. Its coarse fur made fantastic waterproof footwear; its bladder could be used to make water carriers; tusks could make weapons, eating utensils or containers; its muscle fibres would be weaved together to create cordage which had a great many uses and its great bones used to make shelters, weapons and needles. It was a great find as they were few and far between in this area now. A must for the tribe.

Quickly, a discussion was had involving the hunters and anyone else who they felt needed to be involved. Affeyso walked around the group, chanting and making hand gestures to the sky and hills around them. Anika knew he was calling on the higher beings to bless the group and thanking them for the opportunity. Another thing this tribe liked to do was ask permission from the animal world to hunt them. This derived from a love and respect of the natural world and all its provision and the tribe deemed it necessary before any big hunt. Anika was stolen away from her thoughts by San's voice as she beckoned to Iwot and herself to join the group. Perplexed, Anika walked over. She had never been involved in a hunting discussion before and was surprised to be summoned.

San spoke directly at her and Iwot, "we need your help," she said, and they sat down within the circle and listened to the plan developing.

Grenn stood, his height was domineering and his beard now much longer after the long trek overland. His skin still tanned from the summer sun.

"Right, does everyone know their role?" he asked.

"Yes," the group replied assuredly.

"Then let's do this," he said as he led the group down the hill and towards the colossal beasts unknowingly drinking on the river's edge.

When Anika looked back on that day later in her life, she was amazed at the skill of this tribe and her heart throbbed with pride at the memory of them and how they worked together to provide for all. It was the only way to survive. A man that only strived for himself would die sooner. It hadn't been the fact that they had hunted a mighty beast but how they had meticulously worked together.

Grenn and the other men had noticed a valley running away from the river but still stuck between two hills. Scouts were sent ahead to see where the valley ended and found it stopped abruptly only a mile in. It led to another hill that rose steeply along small tracks, the rest was covered in bracken. Observations of the mammoth showed they were moving slowly and would pass the nook in the hills just as night fell. Swiftly and skilfully, torches were created from the burning ember still being carried by Affeyso. These were passed around the older children who had been chosen for this particular task. Iwot led them down the hill and they positioned themselves further down the river whilst some of them went up river just past the nook, adrenaline pumping as they waited.

Lonn, Sonq and the other tribesmen, whose skill was with the bow and arrow, retreated down the nook and took position on the sides of the hill. Grenn continued up the nook and waited amongst the bracken with Stol and twenty other hunters all armed with spears. Then they waited. Each one anticipating the setting of the sun and knowing the importance of timing in this particular situation. Then it came, out of the sky on top of the tallest hill, the sound of the horn. Affeyso stood there, cloak blowing in the wind, lips to the Rhino's horn he carried with him everywhere and blew.

"Ready everyone?" Iwot called until his voice was drowned out by the sound of pounding. It was a terrifying noise and for a moment made Anika wish she wasn't there, but then she saw the others begin to move and she followed, adrenaline filling every inch of her body. Standing within metres of the charging herd, the children waited – the youngest of which were Tolli and his playmate Sky both just shy of thirty-two seasons. They watched intently as the herd of mammoth charged past them, spooked by the sound of the horn. Dust covered everything around them as they churned it up with their feet, creating a cloud above them. Due to this, Affeyso and the women with small children (including San) stood up on the top of the hill, couldn't see the children on the edge waiting for their moment. As predicted, the small group of mammoth that had separated themselves from the rest were further behind and there was a gap between the main herd and them. Iwot ran slightly further up the hill for a better view of the stragglers behind. Only five remained, three fully grown ones at the front and at the back was the baby plus another adult who on closer inspection seemed elderly and wasn't much faster than the baby. He jumped back down the hill to the others, almost stumbling. The look of alarm on his face concerned Anika who had come to know all his facial expressions well.

"There's two of them," he spoke rapidly in-between short intakes of breath, "they haven't separated. The baby and an elderly one."

"What do we do?" Tred questioned, his brown eyes penetrating Iwot waiting for an answer. Only then did Iwot realise the position he was in. He was the oldest, age was an important thing in the tribe. With age, came wisdom. No matter the gender of the people involved, the oldest present at the time would make the decisions for the group they were with.

For a very brief moment, Iwot allowed himself to be overwhelmed with the weight of the decision upon him and then he made it. With conviction, he yelled, "we go, torches held high, voices loud. Let's move." He jumped down into the now well-trod path of the last two mammoths, everyone followed.

Unsurprisingly, the noise they created could be heard from the top of the hill even if they were still unable to see what was happening. There was no time for Anika to look around her and view who was there but she could feel them. Every child between the ages of seven and twelve were down there, torches in hand – shouting and screaming at the top of their lungs and waving their arms. It made quite a ruckus and was more than enough to persuade the two charging mammoths to halt their approach, turn around and begin again in the other direction. As instructed, the children followed, still yelling and brandishing their torches – the animal's fear of fire working to their advantage. Further along the track, just after the nook that the hunters were waiting down, with growing anticipation, were the women of the tribe who weren't being used as hunters. They had the same role as the children in attempting to divert the mammoths off their current path and into the nook. It worked well and the mammoths set off down the nook, terrified into hysterics by the organised chaos all around them. Suddenly, Anika heard a scream and watched as Sky who had gotten too close to the back of the turning beast, disappeared under the back feet of the giant creature.

Iwot saw Anika stall in her march behind the mammoth, "Anika, keep going!" he yelled.

"But Sky," she pointed to the bundle still on the ground behind them.

Iwot grabbed her by the arm, "the mothers will see to her, we have a task to complete."

She knew he was right, so with one last glimpse behind her at the still form, she continued following the mammoth to ensure they didn't turn back around. Up ahead, Anika joined the women and children in the next step of the plan. As the mammoths wound their way up the nook, the tribe moved the bundles prepared earlier across the valley entrance about two-thirds of the way in. As soon as they were ready, they spread out across the valley and bent down with their torches. All of a sudden, they were distracted by a petrifying sound. Having found that the end of the valley was a dead end, the mammoth, as predicted, had turned back around once again and were now heading straight back to the women and the children. With only their torches as light, they couldn't see them but they could hear as their approach became louder and louder. They were stuck, nowhere to run, nowhere to hide from the great pounding feet of the gigantic beasts who would stop for no man. They would be flattened, crushed to the ground beneath them.

"NOW!!" someone yelled, "LIGHT THEM UP!"

Fear filled the voice but there was also the sound of determination. All responded and then watched as the flames took hold, cascading like waves from one pile to another. The flames caught the dry bracken immediately. The noise increased and it seemed like the mammoth were right on top of them and as they watched the last section take hold they could see from the silhouetted giant shape just on the other side of the fire, that they had been. A split second had saved them all. Over their cheering, could be heard the loud trumpeting of the petrified animals as once more they turned and headed back down the valley.

Iwot tugged at her arm, "let's go watch." he said, excitement in his eyes.

Running back up the valley the way they had come, they found a small crevice in the hill that they worked their way through before climbing up and coming out close to the top of the hill. From here, they ran towards the edge that looked over into the nook where they knew the hunters were waiting. Arriving just in time, they watched as the animals began to realise the predicament they were in. The tribe had created a ring, like a stage that the animals couldn't escape from. One after the other, they waited unsure of what was coming.

"What are they waiting for?" Anika asked, wondering why the hunters hadn't struck yet.

Iwot replied, "they were only expecting one mammoth, two causes problems."

Anika nodded her head in understanding.

It all happened very suddenly after that. For a moment, all that could be heard was the loud exhaling of the exhausted animals. Then out of nowhere, ten men jumped from the bracken with loud roars. To Anika, they seemed to fly – many of them landing on the back of the elderly mammoth. Immediately, they plunged in their spears before jumping off, rolling clear of its mighty feet and standing. After which, they would run into the bracken ready for another attempt. The men that didn't make the back of the elderly mammoth, seemed to be on baby mammoth watch. Standing beneath the animal, they yelled and shouted keeping it away from the adult one. During all this commotion, the members of the tribe on the side of the valley hills were using their bows and arrows in an attempt to cause further damage and to bring the mammoth down. Fascinated, Anika watched as Stol, one of the few female hunters, flew from the bushes, grabbed the mammoth's horn as it swiped at the men below it and using the momentum from the swing of the mammoth's head, landing directly on its back where she plunged her spear in. The shot was fatal and the mammoth fell to its knees. For a moment, Anika thought it would crush the men around it but they swiftly sprung to the side before all turned their focus to the baby mammoth. As if it knew, the baby started to run back towards the fire which was still blazing bright. Anika could see Grenn yelling to the others, they followed his orders without question and began to spread out to the sides once again. Just below where Iwot and Anika were standing they watched someone throw something down to the waiting tribe. Further along the valley, the fire was suddenly shadowed by the gigantic form of the mammoth who had made it to the barrier and turned itself back around again. Anika couldn't see who it was or what they had thrown but she watched as the mammoth continued to run back and forth, unsure what to do. Even as a baby, it was almost twice the size of anyone there and they continually scuttled about, moving out of its way.

"Why don't they strike?" she asked Iwot once again.

He didn't turn to her to answer, not wanting to take his eyes off the happenings below for one second, "they are letting it tire itself out so it doesn't have as much energy to fight them."

Finally, it stopped and faced its foe. It roared, trumpeting its protest. Quickly, the tribe took its opportunity and Anika watched as three of them wound their way round and round the animal's hind legs. Once or twice the giant beast turned its head to see what was happening but the men at the front continued to distract as best they could with shouts and screams and stabs of their spears. At Grenn's signal, the men at the front stepped back, dropped their arms and became quiet. Perplexed by this sudden change in tactic, the mammoth gave one loud trumpet then began to march towards them. As soon as his front feet moved forward, the tribe at the back – some good thirty or so men and women - pulled on what Anika could now see was cord. They gripped tightly as the men at the front began to threaten the great beast once more. The more they yelled and screamed the more the beast tried to get to them and the harder the tribe at the back pulled on their cord. Many men were pulled off their feet as the strength of the animal beat them and it almost pulled its legs free. On the edge of the hill, the men with bows and arrows joined the tribe at the back and finding a free space, grasped the cord with all their might and pulled. A minute later, Iwot and Anika made the same decision and followed them down. Also grasping the cord, Anika could feel the coarseness of it biting into her palms as she used all the strength she could muster. With one last groan, the mammoth gave in and collapsed to its knees. Men off to the side, who Anika hadn't noticed up until then, took the opportunity to jump onto the beast's back and make the essential fatal wounds. It slumped to the floor, as did all the men and women around it, the adrenaline tailed off and exhaustion set in. They had done it.

Twelve

Unfortunately, the success of the hunt came at a cost. Little Sky, just seven years old, died of her injuries that same afternoon. The mighty beast had trampled her and there was no way to stop the flow of blood. As usual, the tribe held a short burial then no one spoke of her again. For Anika, this was too much and she lay around the fire that night with tears cascading down her cheeks, as she thought about all the people in her life she hadn't seen and may never see again. All around her, people were engrossed in their tasks. Two Woolly Mammoths were great work for a tribe. Using their tools, made from stone and crafted to a perfect point, they cut through the meat, not wasting any part. Parts of the animals were shared out amongst the tribe and given to those who needed specific things. Finally, the camp grew quiet as all began to rest around the fires. Anika could smell the meat roasting and watched as San and Stol created the fire to smoke to help preserve the meat and make it last longer. As the stars twinkled brightly in the sky, Anika looked to them for help and hope that she would one day find her father again.

Early the following morning, she was woken by Grenn who insisted she eat something. Her thoughts kept returning to Sky but she managed to force down some of the roasted meat along with a handful of wood sorrel. It tasted sour in her mouth and she took a swig of water from Grenn's ostrich egg nearby. Looking around, she realised the camp was quite empty and many of the fires had died down.

"Where is everyone?" she asked.

Grenn stood for a moment and looked around the camp too before replying, "They are scouting mainly. Looking for a place to set up for winter."

Anika stood up and stretched before washing her hands with some water and scooping up the small bones that had been amongst her meat. These could be used she knew to create small tools or as fuel for a fire, "why didn't Iwot wake me?" she questioned.

Grenn stood in front of her, blocking the morning sun. Gently, he placed a hand on her shoulder. "He could see you were upset last night and wanted to leave you to your thoughts."

This irritated Anika somewhat. She knew people shied away from emotion concerning death in this tribe and the fact that Iwot didn't want to talk about Sky with her made her sad, but also angry at what she considered to be the tribe's ridiculous ideas. Suddenly, she kicked at the dirt around the fire, sending gravel and grit towards it.

Watching her closely, Grenn took a deep breath and approached her. He sat down on a log surrounding the fire and gestured to Anika to join him.

"Do you want to talk about it?" Grenn asked her, his voice soft and calm.

Anika stared at him confused, "talk about what?" she asked.

"Whatever is bothering you," Grenn replied.

"I can't, well you all say I can't," she replied, irritation evident in her tone.

Grenn began carving a small lump of stone, attempting to put a point into it to use as a hand axe. "You can Anika. Anything."

Slowly, she turned her head towards him studying him. He didn't look anything like her father – he was dark and her father was blonde, but he had become her father these past months and she was comforted just by his presence beside her.

She began to speak slowly, "I wanted to stay with her. Go back to where she was lying after…well…after the mammoth…hurt her, but Iwot pulled me on, he said the hunt was more important." Tears began to flow down her face again, "how can it be more important than her, than a girl, a person?"

Grenn put down his tools and took Anika's hand before starting to speak, "nothing is more important than life, Anika. Iwot knew the women were watching and would go to Sky as soon as it was safe and they did. She wasn't alone when she left this earth."

"Was she afraid?" Anika asked.

"No, child. Sky believed, as we do, that when we die we go to the great ones in the sky and that one day we will all be together again." He explained as he wiped the tears from her cheeks.

"So why won't you talk about them then? Why won't you speak about your memories, about your time with the people you loved? About your son?" At this,

Grenn took his hand away and stared out across the valley. "I'm sorry," Anika said.

Grenn sighed deeply, "no, Anika. It's ok. He was a fine lad – my first boy. He looked a lot like Dati does, a lot like me. Dark, curly hair that grew fast. He was strong, really strong for such a young boy and he was a fast learner – was so good with a slingshot and he was just learning to hunt with a spear when…well…when he fell."

He picked up his stones again and began carving the edge, after a few seconds he stopped, "he was trying to follow us. We were going on a hunt and he wanted to come with us. I told him he was too young and not ready yet. He insisted he was ready but I wouldn't allow it. But…but he came anyway. Climbed way up high so we wouldn't see him following us then…then," he stopped talking and when Anika turned to him she saw the tears welling in his eyes.

"Grenn," She said.

He continued to speak, quieter now as people were starting to return from their scouting, "he fell from a spot taller than this valley onto the trees. He died instantly – there is that I suppose. He didn't suffer. But…but…he was my boy, my son. I loved him. I miss him." The tears were running freely now into his long beard.

Anika stood up, bent down in front of him before wrapping herself around his shoulders and pulling him close. For a short time, he sobbed in her arms – quietly, as he let go of all the pain and grief that had been bottled up for a long time. After a while, he stopped and pulled himself away.

"Thank you," he said to Anika, "thank you so much." And with that, he got up and walked away.

It wasn't long before a commotion by the main campfire caught Anika's attention and she moved closer to see what was happening. Grenn was there too now and most of the tribe had returned.

"What is it?" she asked Madchen who was sat feeding her youngest child.

"They may have found a shelter for the winter," she replied before lifting her baby onto her shoulder and patting its back. Loudly, it let out a burp as the trapped wind was relieved. Anika smiled at the small bundle before turning back to the discussion being had not far from where she stood.

"Over behind this next hill," Sonq was saying pointing past the hill they were facing.

"It's vast. We haven't been far in but it goes back many metres. There are other smaller caverns off of it and there is a large gorge cut through the rock," Tred continued.

"Is there a river?" Grenn asked.

"Yes, further down the gorge. It seems to flow from out of the ground. Maybe the caves are flooded further in but what we saw looks secure. No sign of animals. We looked for the telltale signs – prints, hair, waste – none to see. It is a beautiful, plentiful place," Tred finished.

"Large enough for the whole tribe?" San asked as she looked around at the many faces amongst them.

"Definitely. There are other caves nearby, not as big but suitable. I think we have stumbled across a network."

Grenn walked towards the men and patted their shoulders, "I trust your judgement. We leave after our midday meal."

There was much excitement as the tribe ate together that lunchtime. Anticipation was high as they wondered about their home for the coming seasons. Anika had been in caves before having used them for shelter. Her mind turned back to one particular set of caves back when she was with her own tribe. It was covered in depictions of animals – fascinating artwork that must have been left by a tribe that had come before them. There were thousands of them, some showed figures too and some more abstract drawings that could have been many things. For hours, she would be sat there with the reflection of the fire, looking at the different pictures and trying to figure out what they were saying.

After packing up their belongings, they began the trek over the hill, once again travelling with the most vulnerable in the centre – always wary of dangers. It didn't take long to get there and it wasn't easy to miss when they walked over the final lip of an amazing gorge. Its cliff rose one hundred and ten metres above the valley and as they stood at the edge, their view of the vast cave below was astounding. It spread across the cliff and its opening was deep, with the lip of the cave providing shelter. From here, they couldn't see how far inside it went but there was also a clear view of at least three other smaller caves dotted along the cliff face.

"It's amazing!" Iwot commented as he stood next to Anika, holding the hands of his younger brothers. He had his bow slung over his shoulder and was carrying a full

Ostrich egg, which he had filled at the last stream they had come across.

Anika replied, "it is that, yes."

"Is this our home for the winter?" Tolli asked, looking across the wide expanse of the gorge to the other side.

"Maybe so, Tolli. Maybe so," Iwot said.

They turned to follow the tribe down the side of the hill into the valley, where they crossed over shrubbery growing wildly and stopped at the cave entrance. Anika watched as Grenn and the other men prepared groups to further explore the caves before they allowed their tribe to enter them fully. Anika watched San, Stol and Madchen work their way around the shrubbery directly in front of the cave. Anika, Iwot and the other older children were left to supervise the smaller ones. Toa, at present, tended to wander off – she wasn't quite at an age yet where she understood all the dangers surrounding her. As Anika watched her toddle off from the fire, she sighed at having to get up once again to return her to the rest of the children. On her way back, with Toa in her arms, she met San.

"Is she playing her games again?" San asked as she tickled Toa under the chin.

"Yes, she is," Anika replied with a smile.

San gestured to the shrubbery around them, "there are many berries, nuts and roots available further down the valley, but this shrubbery we will need to cut back to ensure we can see predators from a good distance.

Anika nodded her head in agreement, this was the first thought she had had when she saw the caves.

At that moment, Grenn returned from inside the cave and nodded at San. His face was smeared with some mud but the smile on it was clear to all. Beckoning to the whole tribe, he walked towards the fire, picking up his daughter Kaie on his way through.

"It is a complex system of caves. The opening is large and perfectly suited to the entire tribe. There is room for family hearths inside and the cave connects to the smaller caves further along. There are many small caverns, perfect for storage of food." He stopped a moment, still in disbelief at their lucky find.

"Further within, dripping through the rocks is a beautifully clear and fresh spring which will provide more than an adequate amount of daily water. The Gods have smiled on us today," he completed his speech and stood for a moment staring into the fire.

"Ok, everyone. Let us prepare," Affeyso spoke.

As soon as he finished his short sentence, the tribe set to work. Families worked together to create family hearths, making fire pits by digging into the ground and collecting firewood. Laying out their animal skins, moss and other soft plant life as beds and setting out their pots, cups and other utensils. Anika joined San, Grenn and their children at their hearth and set about collecting water containers and filling to the brim with the spring water Grenn had spoken about. As she saw the water dripping through the rock, she was amazed at how clear it looked and fresh it tasted but even more astounded by where it came from.

Later in the afternoon, the remainder of the Woolley Mammoth meat was shared out between the families and they were left to do with it as they wished. The tusks had been shared between Sonq, Flur, Grenn and Stol, who had been seen to be the hunters who had given the fatal blow to the giant creature. At present, they were using them as hooks for clothing and bags, but when they moved on, it was likely they would be used to help construct housing. The animal's guts and skin had also been shared between families, so now their task of finding winter shelter was complete, they set about beginning winter tasks. Repairing clothing, making new, carving bowls and cups and making new weapons or tools.

As the evening set in and families began to settle down for the night, Anika watched the activities taking place in the cave around her. Kaie was asleep with her head on Anika's lap and the other smaller children were beginning to sleep. She added some more wood to the fire and watched as the flames lapped around it. Grenn and San were sat on the other side of the fire, their heads touching each other as they whispered. Iwot had disappeared somewhere with his group of friends, exploring the maze of caves she expected and was slightly irritated that she hadn't been invited. It was at times like this, as she nibbled on wood sorrel and hazelnuts, that she thought most about her father. She couldn't believe he was dead, it didn't feel like he was, even though she wasn't sure what that felt like. Memories of his face were beginning to blur and it brought tears to her eyes when she struggled to remember his voice. It had been half a year since the giant waters had attacked her, dragging her into a new existence. She was thankful for the people of the Golden Eagle tribe but for her, making her way home was always on her mind and as soon as she was ready, she would make the journey and return to wherever it was she came from.

Thirteen

The discovery of the caves was an enormous triumph for the tribe. Winter set in fiercely just six weeks later with the first snowstorm. It hit overnight and surrounded the cave in knee-high snowdrifts. Laying close to Kaie and Toa with their body heat radiating, Anika could see the swirling flakes falling but she didn't feel cold. A fire raged through the night, everybody taking the opportunity to add extra fuel whenever they woke up. Collection of firewood became of highest priority and there were stacks of it leaning against every cave wall. Animal skins hung all around also as the tribe attempted to soften them to make them more pliable before using them to make cloaks and other clothing. It was essential that everyone had an animal skin cloak and that there were spares.

As she listened, the wind whistled through the small holes in the windbreak that was making a real difference to the warmth of the cave. It was made out of wood stakes driven into the ground and animal skins laced together with horsehair and sinew. Without it, the cave would become a trap for snow drifts and strong winds. In the last six weeks, all members of the tribe who were capable would spend the large majority of their day hunting, not just for the food but for animal skins to use, to protect them from the weather. This meat was all over the cave – it had been cut into thin pieces and hung deliberately over smoking fires which helped to preserve the meat for longer periods. One of the smaller caverns down a small tunnel was being used to store this meat. It was almost full with the newest smoked meat at the back. There were stores of nuts, green leaves and berries plus piles of stones that people had been gathering ready to begin shaping new tools and weapons, also a winter task.

Kaie rolled over in her sleep, dislodging the animal skin keeping her warm as she did so. Anika moved away from Kaie, replaced the animal skin then stood up and began to walk towards the entrance to the cave. It wasn't quite first light yet and the majority of family groups were still asleep. When Anika reached the windbreak, she stood with her arms wrapped around her wishing she had picked up an extra cloak. Snow had always been fascinating to her, from the moment she first saw it as a small child. Its potential to kill never crossed her mind, she enjoyed the beauty of the silky, smooth coating it gave to everything around it, the crunch it made under her feet and the patterns that formed when it froze, dangling from trees and cliff faces.

"It's a harsh one to start the season," Grenn said as he walked up next to her scratching his beard. He stretched his arms out then moved from foot to foot, stomping his feet. "Nothing worse than feeling cold," he remarked.

Anika smiled, "I don't mind the cold. It makes this seem cosier," she replied directing her hand around the cave.

"It does that I suppose. Though makes it far harder to survive."

"We have plenty of stores," Anika said.

"Yes, plenty but enough, I'm not sure."

Anika surveyed Grenn as he stood rubbing his hands together and staring out into the white mist. His beard had grown even longer and now covered his entire face. Anika always thought how unfair it was that men could do this, create a covering for their faces with little effort that would keep them warm throughout the harsh months. Now, as she watched him, she noticed that he had stopped moving and was staring at something in the snow about ten metres from the windbreak where they were both stood. Her gaze followed his and she immediately noticed what he had spotted. Barely visible through the cascading snow that had settled on top, were some animal prints. They were large and dotted in a circle that moved across the entrance of the cave then back down the side of the valley path next to the cliff.

"What do you think it is?" Anika asked Grenn.

He turned to Anika, "no doubt about it, those are bear prints."

"Bear? But why are they not sleeping?" she asked.

"Not all bears sleep throughout the entire winter Anika, especially if they don't have enough food or haven't fattened up enough over the months before winter." He moved away from the entrance and began to walk towards a family hearth not far from the front of the cave. She watched as Lonn was woken by Grenn with a gentle shake of his shoulder before both men returned to the windbreak and Grenn pointed out his discovery to him.

Anika made her way back towards her fire as she noticed people beginning to stir and she knew San would want some help with the morning tasks. She wasn't sure what Lonn and Grenn were saying but she could tell from their animated conversation that they were both concerned by the discovery Grenn had made.

"Morning Anika. What is it?" San asked, as she too noticed her partner and friend talking.

"Bear prints," Anika replied, as she began to collect drinking containers from around the sleeping children. As she passed Iwot, she gave him a nudge with her foot. He responded with a groan so she nudged him again. As of late, Iwot had become the last to rise from the fire and begin to help with the tasks and it frustrated Anika that he did so. So every morning, she helped him wake up with nudges, pokes and sudden noises that he didn't appreciate but she did it nonetheless. Yesterday, she had set the little ones on him, allowing them to pile on top of him and find areas of exposed skin to tickle. This had been her most successful wake-up attempt, but unfortunately didn't get him to his tasks any quicker as he continued to lie on the floor, rolling around with his siblings, laughing and tickling them back until Toa got squished by Tolli and the result had been a scream followed by crying that had awoken not only Iwot but the entire cave.

"Get off," he mumbled.

"Get up," she responded, before giving him one more nudge and heading in the direction of the spring. Out of the corner of her eye, she noticed Iche heading in the same direction so she quickened her pace ensuring she reached the spring first so she didn't have to queue. Noticing her pace getting faster, he too sped up and they laughed together as they collided trying to make their way through the narrow passage to the cavern the spring was in.

"Ladies first," Iche said with a smirk on his face.

This type of comment always irked Anika as she felt it was Iche's way of suggesting that she needed to go first because she was the weaker of the two.

"Oh no, I insist," she responded, moving aside so he could walk past. As he made to move around her, she sidestepped and blocked his path with her back. He bumped right into her, stumbling over and landing on his bottom.

"Ha," Anika said, "I don't need your help Iche, I am a warrior woman." She pounded her chest then turned and walked away. As she was beginning to fill up the first container, he arrived behind her and sat on the rock waiting for her to finish. The look on his face told her she had been successful at irritating him. She couldn't wait to inform Iwot of her triumph when she returned to the fire. As she filled up the last of the containers and slung them over her shoulder, she once again marvelled at the fact that this water stayed the same temperature all year round, no matter what the weather was outside. The whole cave did in fact, away from the draft of the openings of course. Grenn had told her something about the rock being so thick that it helped to keep the warmth in, but she liked to believe it was magic and that Affeyso had put some spell on the cave that ensured it would remain welcoming to the tribe.

In summer, the temperature would be considered cool but with winter's arrival outside, Anika was more than happy to sit in the cave all day long then trudge around freezing her toes off. There was plenty to fill her days. Yesterday, she had spent the entire time making shoes for the babies who were beginning to toddle around. In the cave, they were considered to be safer and were allowed more freedom. Any wild animal would steer well clear of the fires burning in the cave and the noise from the people and wouldn't venture close enough to be a danger. It surprised Anika how smart the babies were when it came to the fire. They steered clear of it, knowing from an early age how dangerous it could be. Very rarely did children receive burns from falling into one. With deliberate slowness, she capped the last water holder then proceeded to wash her face in the pool formed at the bottom of the spring. This was too much for Iche who sprung up from his crouched position and walked towards her.

"Move it, girl," he said with irritation before nudging her aside and sitting on the little stone ledge. Anika began to uncap the last container she had filled and was about to tip it over Iche's head when…

"Anika," a deep voice resonated around the cavern. She stopped, her hand paused in mid-air and turned to face the voice.

Iche's father stood by the entrance with a stern face although she thought she saw a smile in his eyes.

"Are you finished?" he asked her.

She lowered her hand but not before Iche noticed what she was about to do, he scowled at her in response.

Anika walked quickly away recapping the container, "yes, I'm all done," she replied.

"Good, off you go then. Lots to do today," he patted her on the head as she quickly wove her way through the maze of rock and back to the main cave. Already, a hunting party was preparing to head out. The snow had stopped and they were making the most of the clear skies before the evening set in and it became too cold to be out. Anika set the water containers down and added some wood to the fire, before taking a seat and helping herself to the bowl of nuts and some small fish that had been caught through holes in the ice of the river further down the valley and baked over the fire. In between bites, she took small swigs of the freshwater whilst watching the activity around the cave. Across the cave, at her family's hearth, Stol quickly tied her loose hair into a tight plait then tucked it underneath her hood before wrapping her cloak around her, grabbing her spear and following the men to the entrance. Anika stared after her in admiration. San noticed the look when she returned to the fire with animal skins across her lap.

"Would you like to be a hunter, Anika?" San asked her with a smile and a glance towards the babe on the animal furs who was snoozing quietly.

"Very much, yes. I want to do more than just stitch clothes, gather wood and have babies," from the look in San's eyes, she knew she had offended her slightly as these were the tasks she undertook daily. "I'm sorry, that isn't what I meant. What you do is very important for the survival of the tribe," she looked down, embarrassed.

San smiled at her, "it's ok, Anika. Sometimes the young speak before they think, that doesn't mean they shouldn't, it just means they need to be quick to realise when someone has taken offence."

Anika nodded her head.

"Hunting is a thrilling thing, the adrenaline your body produces when an animal is threatening your life, some people can't cope with it but others thrive on it. It is, however, incredibly dangerous. The number of people we have lost that way…" she stopped, attempting to remove thoughts of dead tribe members from her mind. "You need incredible strength, stamina and skills. Is that still something you want to do?"

"More than ever. Watching the mammoth hunt was the greatest thrill I'd ever had. It took everything I had to hold back from jumping on that mammoth's back myself."

At this, San laughed aloud, "I'm glad you didn't. Well, if it is something you want to do it is important to maintain your fitness and become even stronger. You cannot let winter be an excuse to get lazy, physically."

"What should I do?" she asked, excited now by the prospect of becoming a part of something.

San put the animal skins on the floor and began to fumble around in her belongings. Out of it, she pulled a needle, made from a slim cutting of animal bone. She threaded animal sinew from the basket next to her knee and began to stitch items together.

"There is a group that are exploring the caves. Moving from chamber to chamber. They go every evening. You should go with them, it will strengthen you considerably." San looked towards the girl who had come so suddenly into their lives. "Now off you go. Get your tasks done or you'll be going nowhere."

Immediately, Anika obeyed. Jumping to her feet, she headed off in the direction of Iwot who was preparing fishing equipment. She took one of the spears from his hands and began to lead them towards the river.

Iwot just stared in bewilderment at her, "um, Anika."

She turned to face him.

"Are you planning to walk in the snow in bare feet all day long or just for now?" he asked incredulously.

At this moment, she started to feel the icy surface beneath her toes and the soles of her feet began to go numb. She stared at Iwot. "No, of course not," she said before smiling and heading back into the cave to dress appropriately.

Fourteen

That evening, Anika rushed through her meal and waited anxiously for Iche to collect her, ready to begin this evening's exploration of the caves. Much to her concern, it was Iche's father who was leading the group. She was worried that he would be angry with her for this morning's event between her and Iche. However, he was the one who came across to get her when he and his son had finished their food. With him, he brought two lamps, lit ready against the dark and gloom that became more intense the further they moved away from the moonlight of the night outside. He handed one to her.

"I'm very glad you will be joining us, Anika. I think it will be lovely for you to get to know Iche a little better." At this, he prodded his son forward.

Reluctantly he spoke, "I am glad too." The words were forced out of his mouth, Anika could tell, but she gave him a smile of triumph and stood up. She was wearing her animal skin shoes but realised now that all the others in the group were barefoot. Athir (Iche's father) followed her gaze.

"We find that our grip is much better with our skin. You can feel the curve of the cave and the surface underneath you. Less likely you will fall this way," he said.

At the word 'fall', Anika's heart skipped a beat. She was a good climber, she knew, but within this tribe and her own, many people had been injured, or worse, killed by a great fall.

"Don't worry," Athir said, patting her head, "you are a grand climber. You will be fine." He gestured across the cave to a small waiting group and they all began to move towards the passage that led to the water source. Anika studied the group. There were six of them; Iche, Athir, Iwot, Ti (Sky's older brother), Lonn and Bran. The only one she was unsure of was Bran. Recently, he had returned from his adulthood challenge. For six months, he had been out in the wilderness, surviving on his own. He had returned with a dozen dead and skinned hares, a basket full of nuts and berries and a hand axe, harpoon and spear set for the hunting group. Celebrations were held throughout the night and Anika had watched his proud family embrace him repeatedly. She had, however, noticed that his siblings (of which there were three) were not quite as pleased. Affeyso had watched him quietly from the sidelines, observing his every move and listening to his tales of danger and desperation. He spoke about following the tribe's path from their home in the valley to their abode amongst the caves. How he had come across Cave Lions viciously tearing apart Elk and who he had had to battle with as they attacked him without provocation. According to him, he had seen them off with the use of fire and a spear before finding a river and wading into it waist-deep. At this point, the lions decided not to follow. He had become a master at catching hare with his slingshot and had found a multitude of berry bushes untouched by squirrels and other small animals. As the colder weather progressed, he had sought shelter in small caves and small wooden shelters. Once finding a tangle of tree roots that had formed a shelter of sorts. Here, he had waited out the first big snowstorm before deciding that it was time to rejoin his tribe. To everyone's surprise, he had also mentioned coming across another tribe in the area, smaller than his but native. They had mentioned to him about a tribe gathering taking place the following summer just south of where they were now. This is what he began to speak of as he followed Lonn and Athir through the passage.

"Apparently, it happens every five years. Always in the south, where the sea meets the land. They talked of red rock and the bones of vast creatures. Bigger than the ones we know of today. It is a fertile place, with plenty for all and not inhabited in the wintertime so spring and summer bring an abundance of life," he said, barely stopping for breath.

"It sounds wonderful Bran. But it depends on the decision of the community. Do we necessarily need to travel all that way when we have all we need here?" Lonn responded.

"You aren't understanding me, Lonn," he spoke arrogantly and with little respect, "You don't stay there forever. It is a visit for the summer then you return home before the winter hits." He sighed exasperatedly like he was talking to stupid people, "It is to join with others, learn from them, trade with them, celebrate life together. That kind of thing."

Athir nodded his head, "Yes, I can understand trading and I'm sure there is much to learn from others. It sounds interesting."

Lonn agreed, "Trade and learning would appeal to Grenn."

At this Bran scoffed, "It doesn't really matter what Grenn thinks, he doesn't make decisions alone you know. Although you would think he did." At this, he gestured towards Anika who didn't quite understand his meaning. Iche laughed.

"Thank you, boys," Athir responded.

Suddenly, Bran stopped. Forcing the people behind him to bump one another at the sudden change in pace. He rounded on Athir who had turned to see what the commotion was.

"I am no longer a boy and I do not appreciate being referred to as one. I have done my dues, survived my challenge and rewarded the tribe with plenty. More than some who return. I bring no shame on my parents, I am now a proper man." He puffed out his chest as if this would convince them all. Anika saw he was a strong man, they all were but compared to the mighty hunters of their group his muscles lacked somewhat. Lonn and Athir stood inches above him and their shoulders were broader. They also had far more hair on their faces, Bran was only able to grow a small fluff around his chin and the top of his cheeks.

Athir looked at Lonn briefly, a fleeting gaze that Anika intelligently concluded showed contempt. She didn't know why.

He responded, "My apologies, Bran. You are all man and have proven yourself worthy."

At this, Bran nodded his head then gestured with his hands for the group to continue which they did gladly, escaping the awkwardness of the conversation. Anika was lost in thought for some time, wondering why he had spoken of Grenn that way. They passed by the cavern with their water source and continued along a thin passage where they all had to turn sideways to fit. Surprisingly, she had never noticed it before due to always being concentrated on the spring and filling the containers. It was difficult to fit through without the use of both hands so Athir went first, feeling his way along with his hands and the little amount of light shed by the lamps behind him. He waited halfway along and took the lamp passed to him which he proceeded to throw into the passage to see where it came to an end.

"It looks like it opens up ahead. Pass me the other lamps," he said.

It was as Anika was passing through this passageway that she heard Athir's exclamation, "Wow! What is this?"

Anika tried to hurry but she was stuck behind Iche who was the slowest scrambler she had ever come across. Finally, she reached the space that all six were now stood in. Each person held a lamp and Iche passed hers to her and stood gazing around him. As the flames bounced off the walls of the dark cavern, it revealed a wonder she had only seen once before. Across the wide expanse of the cave they were now stood in, Anika could see pictures – hundreds of them. They seemed to be drawn in red of some kind and were quite simple but beautiful nonetheless. There were pictures of creatures they knew and some they didn't, paintings of figures fighting around what seemed to be fires and others showed them at peace. The ones Anika admired the most were more abstract, such as images that showed the sun, then maybe mountains and other things she was unsure of. For what seemed like an age, they stared before Athir spoke.

"This is a wonderful find. I feel we were led here by the higher beings. Maybe it is a place of worship or thanks for what life brings us," he said.

"Affeyso should see this," Lonn added.

"Most definitely," agreed Athir, "but for now we need to move on, see where these passages lead us." He gestured around the cavern where Anika could now see three other tunnels out of the cavern.

They left the cavern heading for the first passage on the left, which after having got down on all fours to move through, unfortunately, found it was a dead-end and they had to scramble flat-faced backwards to where they began. The second passage led to a thin but tall cavern that looked like it might hit the surface as Bran was sure he could see the stars. On their third try, the passage moved along steadily before forcing them on to all fours and winding for what felt like an age. They had to be careful not to crawl too close to each other so as not to burn each others' toes. After a while, they came to a stop in the tunnel and Anika could hear Lonn, Athir and Bran talking before they finally stopped and made space for the others to crawl out. Once she got to her feet, she could see they stood in a small round cave and then she noticed just a metre in front of her a steep drop. How far she was unsure until

Iwot threw a small stone into the abyss and it took a long while to clatter at the bottom.

"Is that the river down there?" Anika asked when she suddenly recognised the noise that filled the silence she had got used to.

"What else could it be!" Bran replied scornfully, as if what she had asked was ridiculous.

"It is, yes Anika," answered Lonn.

Pointing to a curve in the rock face above the drop Athir began to speak, "we think, if we wedge ourselves into that crevice in the rock's curve there, we can use the grip on our feet to get to the other side."

Iche replied, "there is another side?"

"Yes, see where the light changes in the cave from pitch black to slightly greyer over there. That is solid ground," Athir answered, as he flickered his lamp as close to the edge as he dared, "does everyone think they can do it?"

All nodded, including Anika, who liked to think she could do it, but was unsure.

"Ok, Bran? You first?" he questioned.

Bran, obviously pleased by the chance to show off his newfound adulthood, stepped up to the challenge and scrambled onto the sloping rock. He wedged himself in almost folding his body in half and using his feet and hands carefully moved along the rock. Occasionally, gravel would trickle into the hole and remind everyone of the drop beneath.

"Easy, easy, always have three points of contact," Athir coached.

Finally, he made it to the other side and having gripped his lamp in his mouth the whole way he shone it around the solid ground he had made contact with. His forehead was covered in beads of sweat and his breathing was heavy.

"What do you see?" Lonn asked.

Bran took a moment to take in his surroundings before responding, "there seems to be one way out. It is a passage, but I can stand tall in it. The ledge is large enough for us all."

Lonn went next and made it easily across with skill and agility. After which Iche and Iwot followed. There was a moment when Anika's heart filled with dread as Iwot's foot slipped and he started to panic. Athir's calm words brought him back to his senses and he continued to the end. Iche, too made it without any major mishaps. Then it was Anika's turn. Her heart pounded in her chest and fear almost choked her, but quickly changed to adrenaline when she mentally informed her body that this was happening whether it liked it or not. Athir came next to her and together they began to move slowly along. Feeling every muscle in her body working at once, Anika breathed in and out regularly and felt her heart rapidly catching up with the amount of air she needed. Fascinated, she watched the muscles in her feet grip the surface and quietly grew in confidence. Maybe too much, because as she got close to the edge she became overconfident and moved a foot and a hand simultaneously. The pressure on her other limbs was too much and she lost her hold. As she began to slip towards the darkness she was filled with a sense of peace that at least her death would be a quick one. However, Athir had no such notion as to allow her to fall and he reached out his foot which as she slipped by she felt and in a last-ditch hope grabbed it, hooking her arms around it. She heard a loud groan from Athir who now had the added force of Anika to deal with as he gripped the rock tightly. Lonn had already sprung to action and was holding Iwot's ankles as he crawled towards Anika. Bran and Iche held onto Lonn as he stretched forward, his own body dangerously close to falling. Iwot reached out towards Anika who looked up with a face full of bewilderment that she was still alive.

"Grab my hand," Iwot said.

Anika looked at him but shook her head, "you can't hold me."

"Anika!" Athir spoke loudly and as she looked at him she could see he was under considerable strain.
Iwot moved a couple of inches further forward, "Anika, you know I can."

At this, she did as instructed, loosening one of her arms from around Athir's foot she took hold of Iwot's outstretched hand. As Lonn began to pull Iwot back, Anika instinctively let go with her other hand and began to grip the rock again. All of a sudden, her feet came into contact with the rock and only then did she realise her legs had been dangling over the dark hole. Her heart was beating so fast she thought it would explode right out of her chest. Iwot set his feet on the ledge at the other side and Anika followed.

"You scared me, Anika, that is some drop," Iwot said as he carefully peered over the edge. Following his gaze, Anika took a deep breath and exhaled loudly as she realised the danger she had been in. A sudden thud made Anika turn back and she watched as Athir slumped down to the ledge, he was wet with perspiration and stood for a moment, hands on his knees as he inhaled deeply.

"Who has the water?" He asked in between breaths.

"Here," said Bran as he removed a large Ostrich egg from around his shoulder and removed the pebble plugging the hole.

Athir glugged it down and splashed some on his head after which he turned to Anika.

"Are you ok?" he asked her.

"Yes, all fine," she walked towards him and flung her arms around his shoulders, "thank you," she said.

Athir was slightly taken aback by the affection, having only ever had sons but he responded by hugging her back before standing uproght, handing the water back to Bran and shaking his limbs out.

"Right, enough delay. Let's go," he said.

The group weren't surprised by the quick decision to continue, within their environment they couldn't allow close calls to delay their task at hand.

The tunnel ahead was low for a while but grew taller as they continued to follow it through. After a while, even Lonn (the tallest of them all) was able to stand upright as they carried their torches to show them the way.

"The torches are getting low," Lonn commented as he looked at the flames still burning.

"We have extra tinder but Lonn is right it may not last long," Bran agreed.

All of a sudden, Athir called out, "I see light ahead, just a glimmer but definite light."

"Really?" cried Iwot, who was growing slightly concerned about being left in the cave without light.

Athir walked further forward, "Absolutely, straight ahead."

Continuing to walk, Anika watched her footing. Iche caught her on one occasion though he had grown quiet since the slipping incident. At last, the light became brighter and grew in size as they approached the opening.

She heard the growl of the bear before she saw it. A deep, low growl that protested about being disturbed whilst in slumber. Its shadow was terrifying as it rose on its hind legs and roared louder.

Athir spoke quietly, "Iwot, take Anika and Iche out now. Go around behind us, we will stand here. It won't attack unless we do." He sounded so sure but once again Anika's heart was in her throat as she followed Iwot around, behind the men and towards the light which didn't seem as bright now, but in comparison to the cave was like an early morning sun. Her foot touched snow just outside the small gap to the cave and the crunch seemed so loud that she was sure it would provoke the bear to attack.

"Get them back to our cave, we are the opposite side of our opening." Anika was astounded by his knowledge of where they had come, to her, the cave seemed like a never-ending maze.

Turning around, Anika glimpsed the full moon that was creating the light they had seen from the cave. She turned back and just before Iwot pulled her away, she saw Bran, Lonn and Athir standing tall like giants as they faced off against the largest cave bear she had ever seen.

It took them a while to return to their cave. Even though the moon was full and the night was light, the deep snow made it difficult for them to move quickly. Besides, all three of them were happy to move slowly in the hope that the three men would catch them up and regale them with stories of their battle with the cave Bear. Unfortunately, this was not the case and they re-entered the cave almost five hours after they had begun their exploration. It was nearly morning and the whole cave was asleep. Iche quickly retreated to his family's hearth and Anika watched as he curled up in a ball next to his brother around their fire. Iwot added some sticks to their fire before settling down on his furs. Only Grenn stirred as the two returned to their family circle.

"Hello you two, it's late," he said quietly, so as not to wake the others. "Problems?" he questioned.

Iwot shrugged then responded, "nothing that can't wait till morning," he said knowing that sending more men before a bear wouldn't help, he lay his head down and dozed off.

Anika did the same, slower than Iwot however. Her evening had been full of adventure and as scary as moments had been, she had loved every minute of it and couldn't wait for the next chance to be a part of something that mattered.

Fifteen

The three men returned home tiredly from their battle with the Cave Bear a little after sunrise. The camp was awake and busy but all had heard the story by then, told with different levels of exaggeration by all three children. All the men had scrapes and cuts which were quickly attended to by the medicine women. Bran had a wound on his temple that was the result of him being knocked sideways onto a rock by the bear's great front paws. It was still bleeding heavily when he returned so a rock was put over the fire. Then, when it was hot enough it was placed over the wound. Bran let out a roar when they did this as his skin was being burnt over the wound to seal it and stop it bleeding. Their story was told by Bran.

"It was a huge beast, easily twice a man's height," he spoke in between grimacing as his other wounds were treated. “We attacked simultaneously, trying to take it unawares from all sides.”

Kaie turned to Anika briefly with eyes full of curiosity, “why didn’t they run away?” she asked innocently.

“You never run from a Cave Bear, they are faster than us and can climb trees and even swim I was told. You have to fight to surviv,.” Anika replied.

Kaie nodded her head and turned back to the story.

“We were battling it for what seemed like ages. I managed to get in some good shots before it knocked me sideways. The force of the blow to my head knocked me unconscious,” he finished.

“So, you didn’t see the rest of the fight?” Iwot questioned.

“No, but it was pretty much over by then,” Bran replied arrogantly.

Lonn and Athir smiled at each other across the fire as they listened to the young man recall his story. It hadn’t quite happened as he said, Bran had been knocked unconscious almost immediately and the other men had succeeded in wounding the animal enough for it to flee into the wild outside the cave. They then took this opportunity to pick up Bran and carried him over half the way back to the cave on their shoulders. However, they didn't contradict his story, knowing that at his age he needed to add brave tales to his list of triumphs to increase his prestige in the camp.

"So, Lonn and Athir saw the bear off then?" Iwot asked. Grenn could see that Iwot was deliberately trying to catch Bran out and although it was a dangerous game to play with a man such as Bran, it reminded him of his oldest son and made him smile.

"No, I just said, the fight was almost over anyway," he glared at Iwot, who was smirking across the fire at Iche who had also cottoned on to what Iwot was doing. "At least I didn't run back to mummy as soon as the danger appeared," Bran added.

"Ok, boys that's enough. We thank all three men for their bravery. Hopefully, the bear has had enough from us humans for the present time and won't venture so closely anymore." Affeyso spoke with authority.

Bran stood up and walked towards his family's circle, holding the compress in place over his head.

Grenn patted his son on the head and indicated for him to follow across the cave. The day was running on and there was still lots to be done.

Over many days that winter, Anika heard Bran retell his story, always exaggerating his role in the whole event. Not only this but he also told many tales about his time alone in the wild. How he had hunted many large animals on his own and survived through torrential rains, horrific storms and burning heat with little shelter. Anika's original dislike for him grew daily as she listened to his boasting and the way he spoke to anyone he considered to be not as bold, brave or as important as he was. At times, she struggled with the cave exploration as he was so rude to his elders and treated the younger ones like they were stupid. Iwot struggled most. He had recently passed his eleventh collection of seasons so he was barely five years younger than Bran which wasn't considered to be much. However, Anika couldn't contain her excitement at the thought of attending the summer festival Bran kept speaking of. It had been discussed at the community meeting and many felt it was too soon to plan such a journey, but the possibility of attending the next one was high. Bran, however, had announced to the whole camp that he would go alone to the festival this year, as he didn't want to wait for the next one which was five years from now. As Bran was now considered to be a man, he could make his own decisions and some were even encouraging him to go, especially his younger siblings. Anika knew there were reasons behind this that Bran didn't grasp and it made her smile whenever she heard someone telling him what a good idea it would be. She too loved the sound of Bran being away from camp for part of spring, all of summer and part of autumn as it would take him this long to travel there and back being that it was a very long way.

Their discoveries of the caves continued and Anika became stronger, faster and a far better climber as she daily took on the tangles beneath the land. There were many more exits from the maze underground and they even managed to find a way down to the underground river and many more caverns, tunnels and winding passageways. When they returned, they sketched the route out in the earth and added to it each day. By the end of the winter, when small shoots could be seen poking through the melting snow and the tweets of birds could be heard as they left their winter homes, the map of the cave system etched into the ground was vast. Others had begun to follow it, winding their way in and out of the cave in different directions depending on where they wanted to go.

Anika loved the spring, it was her favourite season. It was just about possible to feel the heat of the sun and she loved to watch the trees, bushes and the ground come alive with fresh life. It also meant their meagre rations could come to an end although just yesterday Iwot had found a group of hibernating hedgehogs and San had cooked up a delightful meal with them as the meat. A pool of water began to form below the lip of the cave as the snow melted off the hill above. Anika liked to watch the younger children as they ran beneath it trying to avoid the drips on their heads. She knew that the cold weather had come to an end when Dati and Tolli ran into the cave one day with a nest full of eggs. If the birds were laying eggs, she thought, the winter must be over. Eggs were a rare treat but always enjoyed by all.

Time continued and for the next two weeks the camp was a thrive of activity as they began collecting young shoots and roots to bulk out their stores and as animals came out of hibernation the hunters would disappear for hours on end and return with a variety of animals. Anika's favourite was wild boar which had a wonderful taste to it especially if they took the time to smoke it and add flavours.

One day, almost at the end of spring she noticed Bran packing up and putting on his travelling clothes – he was off to his festival. She was a part of the group that saw him off, all of which (except his parents), were pleased to see the back of him even if it was only for a short time.

By mid-summer, the fruits were in bloom and Anika spent her days collecting wild plums, gooseberry, lowbush blueberries, deerberry, raspberry and later on blackberries. The cave had baskets full of them. Many were eaten daily to supplement meals but some were fermented with honey and used to make a drink Anika found far too bitter for her tastes, but it made people do silly things and the cave was always full of laughter when people were drinking it. The added sweetness in her diet always put her in a good mood and this was how Grenn found her one evening just after dinner. With the baby on her lap (who was almost two and would need a name soon), Anika was eating a small pile of wild strawberries that she had collected earlier that day with Iwot.

"Has he had some of those too?" Grenn asked pointing to the baby who was slowly closing his eyes on Anika's lap.

"Not many, I remembered they sometimes upset his tummy," she replied.

Grenn sat down on the animal skin next to her, "we have been talking, I and the hunters, and we think it is time for you and Iwot to join us."

Anika almost jumped out of her seat before remembering she had a snoozing baby on her lap.
"Really? That's great! I know I can be of help to you."

Grenn put his hand on her arm, "Iwot too, just remember to listen and follow all instructions immediately. We will be heading out tomorrow morning first light. There is a vast herd of red deer in the next valley we have had our sights on for a while."

"I'll be there," Anika responded.

Grenn chuckled, "I know you will."

Throughout the night, Anika found it difficult to sleep. Her excitement bubbled up inside her every time she thought about being a part of a proper hunt. Since the night she had watched the brave men and women defeat the mammoth, her only wish was to be a part of such a battle.

"Anika, you need to sleep or you will be useless to everyone," San commented to Anika as she watched her tossing and turning upon her animal skin.

Anika turned to face her, "I'm sorry, I am struggling to sleep tonight."

"I can see that, but you must," San replied.

"You're right," she said and with that, she rolled over and attempted to fall asleep once again, but her dreams were filled with the mammoth hunt and the look in Stol's eye when she dealt the ultimate blow to the struggling animal.

As soon as the sun appeared that morning, Anika was up and busy. She set about ensuring her travelling bag had enough food and water in it. She also packed moss, bandage leaves and other essentials needed for on the spot medical treatment. Out of the corner of her eye, she saw Iwot put his sling in his bag with several perfectly shaped stones ready for use. She did the same. Grenn was awake long before her and he returned from the entrance of the cave where he was watching the sunrise and motioned for Iwot and Anika to join him.

"The valley is across those two hills and over, it is a unique spot, there is a great water to the West but I can't tell how far." He gestured with his arm and Anika took in the hills they would be climbing that day.

The hunting party consisted of thirty or so people and only three of those were women. Anika didn't understand why more women didn't want to be a part of this. San had spoken to her about a women's role in the tribe and how, without women, the tribe wouldn't continue. But all of this was of little interest to Anika, having just past her ninth group of seasons, she still found boys of high irritation and was not at all interested in finding one she wanted to settle with. Adventure was what she thrived upon and her life within the tribe allowed for plenty of this and she loved it.

"Are you frightened?" Iwot asked her as he dropped back to walk with her.

"A little maybe, but more excited really," she replied.

"I'm not scared of course," he said puffing up his chest and holding his spear high.

Each of them had been taught to hold, carry and throw a spear plus using it to stab with. They had become quite good and confident now to use it on larger animals.

"Of course not, how could you be?" Anika replied with a smile on her lips. It amazed her that men could not admit when they were afraid. In her mind, it made a person stronger if they admitted their fears but didn't allow them to overwhelm or flood them.

Iwot turned his head at Anika's sarcastic tone but chose to refrain from answering back, having been warned by Grenn that if they started bickering, as they did at home, he would make them return before the hunt.

In Anika's mind, the sun had risen high by the time they reached the top of the hill above the valley where the deer were said to be. Grenn stopped the group and sent only Lonn and Stol ahead to scout the area. Everybody else sat on rocks and grass and had their midday meal. San had provided her with some cold Hedgehog meat, which was far less appetising than when it was warm, but she ate it with some plums and wild parsnip before swilling it down with some water.

Stol and Lonn returned swiftly and talked with Grenn before joining the rest of the group.

"The deer are still there, plenty of them drinking at the river. The easiest way to hunt them is with a bow and arrow then spear holders should pounce for the final blow. One group will approach from the left, one from the right and one dead centre. We aim to gather as many as possible. Let's go," Grenn said.

Anika and Iwot followed the right group with spears in hand. Both had been learning how to use a bow and arrow but as yet weren't quite good enough with it to use it in a hunt. She watched as the three groups passed through the long grass like a swarm of bees. They moved fast and were meticulous in their choice of route, ensuring that they came at the deer from all sides. Swiftly, they approached the valley and just as the great Elk did when Anika had approached it in the forest over a year ago, they began to sniff the air as soon as it seemed to smell strange. Their ears pricked up and moved around as the wind carried the human whiff deer had grown used to avoiding. Unfortunately for the deer, they realised seconds too late and as they began to flee, Anika and her tribe ploughed down the hill and directly blocked every path they could leave from. In their fear, some attempted to cross the river behind them but were quickly stopped by the strong currents caused by the heavy rains days before. The hunters yelled their tribal calls and as arrows began to fly, Anika let up a cry of her own thanking the gods for this opportunity. She watched as close by, Iwot plunged his spear into the belly of a deer brought down by arrows. Not long after, her time came and she too gave the fatal blow to two deer in succession. The tribe left the valley with twelve deer slung across their backs. Iwot smiled at Anika as they walked back over the hills. She had a smear of blood across her cheek and her eyes were full, he wasn't sure what of, but he had never seen her looking so happy.

"That was amazing!" he said to her.

She sighed, a tired but happy sigh, "yes, it was."

Catching up with the both of them, Grenn patted them on the back. "You mustn't forget to thank the gods and the animal kingdom for feeding the tribe. Without their permission, we would go hungry."

They both nodded their heads in response.

"Good work out there today, I am mighty proud of you both," he said before heading on to Stol who handed her deer to him having carried it part of the way back. Anika watched the woman closely, today her hair was tied in a plait that weaved its way from the front to the back of her head and fell down her back. Since losing her husband, she had only become stronger and she inspired Anika to be more than just a woman for a man or a mother for children. She wanted to make a real impact on her tribe, she wanted to be remembered.

Sixteen

For the following five years, the tribe stayed where they were. Normally they would move on after surviving through the winter but the area was more than plentiful, with fertile lands, bushes, grasses and rivers that produced bounties over and over again, there was no reason for them to go anywhere. Some of the tribe had made the trip to the coast which could be seen on the horizon and returned with tales of great species swimming offshore and swamps full of water that tasted salty. Anika had no desire to leave the caves – her discoveries within them were enticing enough and she enjoyed the daily routine of the cave. Winter's were cold but cosy and the spring seemed to come quicker every year and summer lasted longer.

Two years before, Iwot had left the cave for his journey to adulthood and returned successfully four months later, bringing with him the pelt of a Cave Lion. He had become a very successful hunter and was a master with bow, spear and slingshot. His relationship with Bran continued to be troublesome as they both fought for respect and position within the cave. However, Iwot was far better at gaining it through kindness and generosity whereas Bran used fear. Anika liked Bran less and less the older he became. His visit to the festival had been triumphant and he returned with new members for the tribe who had useful skills that the tribe welcomed.

This spring, all members of the tribe apart from the old, very young or infirm were intending to follow him south to join the festival. All around her, the tribe were packing their belongings – choosing wisely what to take so as not to overload themselves. Anika herself was also packing and was looking around the campfire for the lid to her Ostrich egg when Han walked towards her, holding hands with Drenna who had stumbled to her little feet just before the start of the previous winter. Han was the name given to Grenn and San's baby when he had passed two collections of seasons. Drenna was Grenn and San's latest child who San had borne two years before. In between these two, San had lost a child in childbirth and almost died herself. Once again, the medicine woman had prevailed and prevented San from dying. This only convinced Anika more that she never wanted children of her own.

"Hello, you two. What are you up to?" she asked with a smile on her face as she noticed the raspberry juice around their mouths.

"We pick basperries," Drenna replied, "ots and ots."

"Did any of them make it into the basket?" Anika asked.

"Not many," said San as she came up behind them. Iwot followed, he was attempting to grow a beard on his face and it made Anika laugh as she saw how little there was considering the length of time he had been growing it.

"What's so funny?" he asked her.

"Just wondering how long you had been growing that fluff on your chin now?" she joked, "Over a year isn't it?"

Iwot scowled at her, "only a few weeks actually and it is growing well."

"Just in time for the summer when it gets hot, hey Iwot?" she chuckled and then laughed harder when Drenna joined in.

"You can laugh all you like but I am a man, officially. You can never be that!"

"Never be what?" she asked genuinely confused.

"A man!" he exclaimed.

"Why would I want to be?" she asked.

"Because you know that no matter what you do and how you act, you can never be as strong, wise and powerful as a man." He laughed at her, "You are merely a woman."

"Iwot!" San warned.

He ignored his mother, "just a little woman" he began to walk away. As he did, Anika reached for her slingshot, filled it with a small stone and flung it at the back of his head. It struck, as she had wanted it to.

Iwot cried out in pain and turned towards her.

"Now who's squealing like a girl?" she said angrily.

"Anika, Iwot, enough!" yelled San, closely followed by Grenn who had watched the altercation from the front of the cave. San approached Iwot and checked his head, she removed her hand from the back of it and showed Anika blood. Immediately, she regretted her actions, not wanting to hurt him but his words had stung.

"I'm sorry," she mumbled before she collected her water container and headed out to the river to fill it up.

Not long after, Grenn joined her.

"Anika, you have to learn to control that temper of yours. You will always come across people who say things that irritate you. You need to learn to brush it off," he said, as he crouched down by the riverside next to her.

She picked up some small pebbles and threw them into the water and watched the ripples they made, some little fish swam up to see what the commotion was in their habitat.

"He always says exactly what I hate to hear," she commented.

"I know Anika, but you show no control when you respond as you do."

"I want to be something more than just a mother or wife," she commented, as tears sprung to her eyes.

Grenn was thoughtful for a moment, "being those things is essential to the survival of our people, they hold high-value, Anika, and shouldn't be frowned upon."

"I know that and I don't want to offend anyone but I want to be more than that. I want to *really* contribute."

"And you do. I see great things in your future, child, and so does Iwot and all the other young men in this tribe. Your skill and strength threaten them not just because you are a girl but because you are an equal."

Surprised, Anika looked up at him expecting to see that he was joking with her. She had never considered herself to be equal to the boys the same age as her before.

"You're right," she said, "I am as good as any of them, I don't need to prove it, they can see it."

Grenn smiled at her, "You are an amazing person Anika, your father would be very proud."

Anika smiled, her image of his face had blurred further now but she could still see him.

"Yes…yes, he would."

They left that same day, saying goodbye to those staying behind. San was one of those along with Madchen who both had children under the age of five. Han and Drenna would stay with their mother. Affeyso wasn't making the journey this time as he considered himself to be getting on in years and wanted to stay in the comfort of his cave. Among them, were at least twenty people who had decided to stay back. Each one was very capable of looking after themselves so the camp wasn't worried about those who stayed. They would be gone for at least four months.

San ruffled the hair of what she considered to be her two oldest children, "be good both of you, a help to your father and keep an eye out for the little ones," she said.

"I am not little!" said a small voice from behind San's legs. Toa spoke up quietly. She was eight years now, the same age Anika had been when she had been found by Iwot. With long blonde hair, constantly blowing across her face and sticky with mud or raspberry juice, San regularly commented on how similar to Anika she was although of no blood relation.

"No, you are not. Not anymore. Have you been practising with that slingshot?" Anika asked her.
To prove she had, Toa produced it from behind her back, loaded it with a small pebble and fired it towards the wooden post holding the windbreak in front of the cave. She hit it dead on.

"Excellent!" Anika commented, "now make sure you stay the best by practising every day. Kill a few hares or birds for the fire – keep everyone fed."

"Of course," Toa said, as she collected more pebbles from the ground around her, putting them in her travelling bag..

Lonn, who was standing with his back to the group sounded the horn which meant it was time to set off. Bran was leading the way along with his friend he had brought back with him the last time who was looking forward to seeing the family she had left behind on the southern coast. As the crowd started to move, Anika followed with one last look at San and the little ones behind her. The last time she had walked away from someone she loved, she had never seen them again so she was understandably apprehensive about this journey.

Iwot put his arm around her, "don't worry, we'll see them soon. Think ahead Anika, it's going to be an interesting summer." He smiled at her before stepping up his pace and finding his friends who were further in front. It was a beautifully sunny day and the sky was blue all around them.

This was what greeted them when they finally made their way to the South coast of this great land they were on. The ocean, blue as the sky; some of the tribe had never seen it before and even though Anika had seen the great waters it hadn't seemed as vast as the expanse she was viewing now. From the top of the cliff they were now stood on, they could see for miles across glistening blue waters that shone brightly. Dati and Tolli were fascinated by the waves as they crashed against the rocks below them. Tred warned them of the strength of these frothing waters and made them promise not to go near them without an adult. All of a sudden, a sound drifted towards them, above the swell of the waves.

"What is that?" Anika asked Grenn.

Walking further along the cliff, he moved over a ridge in the hill and then stood stock-still. Anika followed him and the view that she saw was astounding.

Grenn swept his arm across the expanse in front of them, "that is the sound of a thousand people!" he exclaimed.

The hill flattened off into a kind of plateau and covering every inch of it, from the cliffside to the valley at the bottom were people. Stood around fires; skinning animals; eating nuts; some were practising with spears; others chatting; some were dancing – moving around to the beat of a drum made using animal skin stretched across a hollow tree trunk. Fascination filled her every bone, she had never seen so many people in one place before.

Bran walked up next to her, "I told you it was worth a visit," he said as he began to walk towards the crowds, pulled forward by his friend who wanted to see if her family were there.

"Unbelievable,"Grenn said staring at the sights around him, "utterly unbelievable."

This wasn't the first time Grenn and the tribe had seen other people but this many in one spot – so many people altogether was shocking to them all.

"Well, let's get set up," Lonn said and began to lead the way down towards the crowds. Anika followed on the heels of Grenn, scared to get lost amongst all these strangers. People were polite and smiled as they went by. Right in what seemed to be the middle of the area, was a huge fire burning fiercely. Around which, huge slabs of meat were cooking and on the floor she could see stones which seemed to be steaming, she was unsure what these were. Lonn had stopped next to a man who was dressed like Affeyso. He spoke animatedly and directed Lonn through the crowds where after walking slightly further, they finally made their way to an empty part of the greenery.

"We can set up camp here," Lonn said, "he is the wise man of a tribe East of here. They come every festival and say there seem to be more people each year."

Anika listened, as she set out her animal skins on the floor near where Grenn and Iwot were making the beginnings of a fire pit.

"That is interesting," Grenn replied, "there are certainly more people here than I have ever seen before in my life."

"It shall be an interesting summer," Lonn stated, before heading off to his own family and beginning to set out his summer home.

That evening, a feast was prepared. The tribe soon realised that everyone cooked food on their hearths then shared it at the big fire or they hunted early, prepared the meat and then cooked it over the central fire for all to share. Anika was sitting on a log near the main fire when some ladies from another tribe began to lift the stones that were earlier steaming. They removed bundles that she could see were wrapped in green leaves of some kind. Inside was meat that had been cooked with wild vegetables, garlic and herbs. Anika moved closer.

"How have you cooked that?" she asked.

The youngest of the group, maybe not much older than Anika herself, responded. "We heat the stones on the fire then dig a small pit. The meat is wrapped as you see then we cover it in the hot stones from the fire, then earth goes over that and it cooks it slowly through the day."

"I have never seen that way of cooking before," she replied. As the girl turned back to the meat, she noticed something hanging from her neck it glistened in the sunlight. Anika couldn't help herself and she leant forward and touched it. "So beautiful!" she said.

The girl smiled at her and removed the necklace placing it in her hand, "you can touch it if you like."

"Where did you? How? What is it?" she asked, as she turned it around in her hands. It was orange in colour but clear and she could see her hand through it. It was the most magnificent thing she had ever seen.

"It's Amber," she replied casually. Anika's perplexed face told her that Anika had no idea what that was.

"Amber is found in trees, inside the bark. It is hardened resin. There are many colours from creamy yellow to red. Have you never seen it before?"

"No, I haven't. You make these necklaces out of it. I have only seen necklaces made of bone and sometimes shells," Anika replied still turning it over in her hands.

"There are tribes here who brought some with them to trade and you are on the coast, there are shells galore down on the beach and some beautiful stones with patterns in them. We should take a walk down there tomorrow. I am Shann by the way, from the East. We have travelled far to be here."

"Thank you Shann, I would like that. I am Anika from the Golden Eagle tribe in the hills to the North," Anika replied.

"Lovely to meet you," Shann said.

Anika spent the evening showing everyone she could find within her tribe the Amber from Shann's necklace. Of course, Bran had seen it before and meant to tell everyone about it. Anika chose to ignore him so he couldn't ruin the evening for her. The evening was another new experience for Anika. After the feast which introduced succulent flavours to her palate, the drums were pulled out and some other instruments that Anika hadn't seen before and people began to sing and dance around under the starlight. For a while she just watched but eventually, she was dragged into it and she found herself moving around as she had never done before. Many things in her life had been exciting but she had never experienced fun like this before. Dancing around for no reason other than for fun. The sun was beginning to rise before they went to sleep around their hearths that night. It felt wrong to be going to bed at the time they normally awoke, almost like they were being lazy, but Grenn did too so everyone followed.

About midday, Anika arose and, after eating a small amount of dried meat, she followed Shann down to the beach. There was a small steep path that opened onto the rocks below. She turned and stared up at the cliff they had come down. It was red, she had never seen rock like it before. Shann was right about the shells. They were spread across the coast. There were small ones the size of a fingernail and ones as large as the palm of your hand. Anika used her cloak to collect them and after about an hour had so many she was unsure she would be able to scramble back up the cliff with them. Just before she was about to leave, Shann began to remove her shoes and wade into the water.

Anika called from the side, "Can you swim?" She asked.

"I'm not sure," Shann called but she continued to wade in as the water splashed against her, "come on!"

+Anika swallowed hard, fear was welling up in her throat but she didn't want to let it stop her from doing something she had always wanted. She took off her shoes and began to wade towards her. The feeling of the sand as it retreated with the water was so unusual she giggled at the feel of it. As the first waves crashed against her, the chill on her skin was a shock but the sun was burning brightly overhead so after a while it became refreshing. She reached Shann and they held hands, bobbing with each wave. Slowly, they made their way further in. The water was now above waist height and with each wave, their feet came off the surface. They looked at each other, both thinking the same thing and after a moment they put their heads under the water and for a while stayed there before coming back up. Anika's grin covered her face, the feeling of being completely under the water hadn't scared her as much as she thought it would. It had exhilarated her.

After a while, they made their way back to the shore and grabbed their shoes. They walked together up the path then made their way to their separate hearths. Grenn saw Anika coming and smiled at her appearance.

"Have you been in the great water?" he asked.

"Yes, it was wonderful," she replied, "absolutely amazing!" She put her cloak down on the ground and the shells spilt out. Toa saw them and immediately came forward.

"What will you do with those?" she asked.

"Make jewellery. Have you seen the ladies here, they all have necklaces and some of their clothes are beautiful. They are covered in tiny shells and Amber which they say you can get from trees. Grenn, there are tribes here who have some and they wish to trade it." She continued to talk for a while before Grenn was able to get a word in.

"Yes, Anika. We are already talking to the tribes about what we can give each other. I am happy that you are learning and experiencing new things but don't forget your responsibilities to the tribe. We still need to eat," he said.

"Of course, yes I'm sorry. I shall take Toa now and find some birds," she said.

"Thank you, Anika. I shall see you later," Grenn said before moving off in the direction of a group of men comparing weapons and tools.

That summer flew by, Anika made many new friends, learnt to swim in the ocean and her tribe discovered many new things that they could take back with them. Trading took place every day and returning with them was a vast amount of amber and seashells for decoration and to make jewellery with, plus knowledge of how to improve tools and weapons. Everyone agreed it was completely worthwhile coming and even Anika had thanked Bran for the opportunity. He had responded with a grunt.

One day, at the end of the summer, when it had been noticed that some leaves were beginning to turn and the evenings were becoming cooler, Anika had been sitting quietly enjoying the music, which a group were playing around the fire, when she was approached by a young man. He wasn't much older than Iwot, with shaggy brown hair and blue eyes. He was very tall and his legs looked spindly on his body almost like a deer on two legs she thought.

"Hello," he said.

Anika responded, "hello."

He gestured towards the stone next to her, "do you mind if I sit?" he said.

"Of course not."

"I was talking to a friend of yours the other day, Iche, is it?"

Anika smiled, "yes, though I'm not sure he would consider himself my friend."

"He speaks very highly of you," he replied.

Anika looked at him in surprise. In all the time she had been climbing and exploring the caves with Iche, she had got to know him quite well but they still bickered almost every day and the competition between them hadn't let off even when they had gotten older.

"He said, and I quote, 'she's pretty good for a girl', he likes you Anika."

She didn't know how to respond to this so she bent her head and waited for him to continue talking.

"Anyway, he told me the story of how you came to be a part of their tribe. You were washed up in the wild wave?" he asked.

Thinking of that day still made her shudder, the freezing water lapping over her body and the exhaustion of trying to stay afloat. Automatically, her hand went to the scar on her stomach.

"Yes, I was. It was a horrible day," she replied quietly.

"Our tribe are from the East and we saw the wave that day. We were on the hills around the flatland and saw it as it raced through. It was an astounding sight even from far away. It washed everything in its path," he said.

"It seemed to come from nowhere," Anika recalled, "one minute I was on the sand by the shallow water and the next I was in it, being washed away, along with the current. I couldn't see my Papa or hear him. I don't know if he could hear me, I was screaming for a long time, whenever my head wasn't under the water."

She took a deep breath and wound her fingers around the necklace she had made recently from small shells.

"The funniest thing about it though, really strange in fact," he said as he thought back to that day.

Anika looked at him, he was staring into the distance like he could see the wave.

"What?" Anika asked, intrigued.

"The water, it never retreated," he replied.

"What do you mean?"

He looked right at her, "the water, that came that day. It never went away. Well, it did, a bit but it covered up the land between the waters."

Anika's heart was pumping, "lands between the waters, what, what is that?"

"Well, my father said that his tribe came across a land bridge where there was water on both sides – miles apart but there. When the wave came it covered the land bridge and never retreated. So, the way my father came is now covered in water. Splitting off one piece of land from another."

Anika's understanding of his words was clear but she couldn't take it in. Tears formed in her eyes as she pictured the last time she had seen her father.

"I can't get back?" she asked this stranger quietly as the tears started to escape down her cheeks.

Seventeen

When the time came to leave the summer festival, Anika had already made up her mind and there was little anyone could do to convince her otherwise.

"You mean to do this?" Grenn said.

"Yes," answered Anika.

"And there is nothing I can say to change your mind?"

"No," she said, "Gre's tribe are travelling to the East, almost to the coast he says. I will be safe with them."

"I'm just not sure you are ready," Grenn continued.

At this moment, Iwot appeared. He had been fishing with his brothers ready for lunch as they began to journey home.

"I will go with her," he said.

Grenn stared at him and Anika could see the look of surprise on his face.

"You don't need to do that," she said.

"I know, but I want to. Can't let you girls go wandering around by yourself," he remarked, then quickly held up a hand to indicate to Anika that he was only joking, "it will be an adventure."

Grenn walked towards him, looking at him for what seemed an age. Then he pulled him into his arms and held him tight. At first, Iwot was surprised but then he relaxed into his father's arms and hugged him back. When he released him, Anika noticed he was crying.

"Your mother will kill me when she sees you aren't here. I promised her I would bring you both back," he chuckled at the thought of San and how mad she would be at him.

The realisation hit Anika all of a sudden that she was leaving the only mother she had known, "can't we go back that way and say goodbye before we go on?" she asked.

"No Anika, it adds a lot of extra miles to your journey. I can't imagine the tribe you are travelling with wanting to take that large a detour," Grenn replied.

All around them, the tribes were packing up and some were even starting their return journey home. It was another sunny day, though not as warm as the weeks previous.

"We can come back though, see her again," Iwot said, as he also thought about his younger siblings.

Shaking his head, Grenn sat both of them down in front of him. "If you make this journey now, you may never be able to return. It is a long way and you will need to stop for winter before you get there." He took both their hands in his, "you may not return, ever," he said solemnly.

Iwot stood up and shook his head, triggering a memory in his father's mind of his oldest son.

"I don't agree father, I know we will return. Tell mother and the little ones, their big brother will be back," Iwot said proudly.

Anika, however, sat quietly contemplating what Grenn had just said. Her eyes were brimming with tears that fell quietly down her face. "I am sorry Grenn, so sorry for doing this. But, well, I have to. I have to know."

Grenn took her face in his hands and kissed her on the forehead for a long time before looking at her again. "Whether you find your father or not, Anika, you will always be my little girl." And with that, he stood up and gestured to his other children who had realised there was something up and had been lurking around in the background for some time.

"Anika and Iwot are leaving us. They are going to be travelling with another tribe for a while – see what is out there," he waved his hand towards the direction they would be travelling in, "say your goodbyes then we must be on our way."

Kaie and Toa ran for Anika and hugged her tightly. Over their heads, Anika watched as Grenn hugged his oldest living son one more time before talking to him swiftly like he was imparting as much as he could about life before he left.

Dati approached Anika, "I hope you find your father," he said, having astutely figured out that that was where they must be going.

Anika nodded, "I hope so too," she responded, before grabbing Tolli and forcing him to hug her before he ran off.

Iwot hugged all his siblings in one big group hug before sending them all off so they wouldn't see him cry. Anika went towards him and squeezed his hand, "Thank you," she said.

He just nodded.

Iche came along at that moment and shook hands with Iwot before coming towards Anika.

He coughed before looking at her then averting his eyes to the floor, "I want you to know that I think you can achieve anything you put your mind to. You are the strongest girl I have ever met and if you want to find your father, I know you will." He walked away. Anika watched him for a while confused by his sudden kindness towards her.

"Let's go," said Iwot as he spied Gre's tribe heading out.

As they walked away, both of them looked behind them for a last glimpse of Grenn. He waved then turned back to his task. They headed over the hills and as they topped the crescent, they both stopped knowing this was probably the last time they would see the tribe of the Golden Eagle. Slowly, Anika held out her hand and as Iwot took it, they began to walk away following their new tribe.

Eighteen

Their journey had many adventures. Winter caught them early, they spent it in small caves only half the way there. Anika and Iwot were useful members of the tribe who were able to catch animals even in the dead of winter when snow was falling and rivers were frozen. They made friends;Gre introduced them to other members of the tribe and they were bringing in enough food and materials to benefit, not just themselves, but others also.

After the winter, as soon as the snow cleared and buds and shoots could be seen, they began their journey again. It was tough going as there were many hills to cross and some large rivers that were swollen by the spring rains. Anika was glad of the swimming skills she had learnt in the sea. However, even she found it tricky to cross a river with strong currents.

One such river perplexed them for many days as they sent scouts up and down to find a way to cross it. The area around it was damp and moist, then after that was swampland before the actual river began. Bursting its banks, it had flooded up and down and the surrounding trees and plants were struggling to cope with the water they were becoming submerged in. The two nights they spent there were cold and damp and it was difficult to keep things dry.

Then one day, Iwot walked up to her as she once again attempted to dry out her shoes by a fire.

"Anika, you should see what they are doing over there. It is simply astounding, I have never seen anything like it," he was excited and spoke fast, spitting out his words.

"What? What is it?" she asked him.

He grabbed her hand, "just come and see."

Pulling her across the swampland, he struggled to walk without falling which made Anika giggle.

Finally, he stopped, "Look," he pointed.

Following his gaze, she saw about ten men working over a large tree trunk. Somehow they had managed to dig out the centre of the tree trunk and were just finishing shaping the front and back so it would glide through the water.

"Where have you learnt to do this?" Anika asked one of the men as he took a break to swig some water.

"It is necessary when you live near water as we have for many years. My father taught me and his father before him," he said, before continuing to scrape the edges with his flintstone.

Later that day, Anika watched as the strongest two swimmers in the tribe swam across, the current taking them quite far down before they walked back up and hooked a line of vines and sinew, that they had been carrying, onto a tree on the other side. There was now a rope of sorts strung just above the flow of the river. Five men piled into the dugout boat and pulled themselves across the river using the rope put up by the swimmers. One of the men then came back for another group. It took over twelve hours to pull the whole tribe across, with some of them having to spend another night on the side whilst they waited for the sun to come up the following day. When Anika and Iwot got their opportunity to sit in the dugout, their curiosity overcame any fear they may have felt. Never before had they seen anything like this, let alone sat in it. Reaching the other side came too soon and they reluctantly got out to allow others to come over.

"I cannot wait to tell father about that," Iwot said. Anika smiled in return. They always spoke about the loved ones they had left behind like they would see them again one day. It was too painful to admit that they might not.

Another month passed before Gre spotted their hill with the valley in between that they had chosen to settle in for the coming months. Having settled in this valley two years before there had been ample opportunity for the plants to grow and it was a fertile land with many resources. Anika noticed a herd of deer in the distance and remembered their location for a future hunt. As they came over the ridge, she saw it. The one thing she had tried to convince herself wasn't there – the great waters. Despair filled her as she slowly accepted the truth and tried to get her head around how this could have happened.

Iwot came up behind her and placed a hand on her shoulder, "I'm sorry Anika. I too was hoping it wasn't true."

Gre saw they had stopped and turned back around to meet them. "The great waters, this is the one that swept you up, Anika. But it never retreated. Stayed there, splitting the land in two."

Anika slumped down to the ground taking the small pebble from her Ostrich egg and having a drink of water. Iwot followed her, knowing that Anika was sipping on her water to ensure she didn't cry.

"I don't know what to say, Anika," he said.

She took a deep breath and stared across the water.

"I'm not giving up Iwot, I will find a way," she said.

"I'm sure you will," he replied, knowing that her stubbornness and perseverance would prevail.

For a moment, they stayed quiet. There was a slight breeze that blew the wisps of Anika's hair and made her shiver slightly before she stood up. She began to follow the rest of the tribe to the valley, where she was shown a shelter of sorts that someone else had vacated over the winter.

"It's not much. It belonged to one of our elderly tribe members but they passed this winter. They had lived many seasons. Unfortunately, the shelter wasn't looked after once its owner left us," he walked around and pointed out the holes in the roof, "you'll need to patch up the holes," he said.

Iwot nodded in agreement, "it's perfect."

Gre laughed, "not quite but I'm sure you two will fix it up soon. You are welcome to stay as long as you like."

And stay they did. Anika spent many days walking up to the top of the hill and staring out across the waters hoping that on a clear day she may see the other side. Whenever Iwot couldn't find her, this is where he would look. Today, he had returned from a big hunt where they had managed to take down four wild boars. He was exhausted but the sun was setting and he liked to ensure she was in the camp before darkness set in. Of course, he would never tell her that, as she would lecture him about her being perfectly capable of taking care of herself. As he reached the peak of the hill, he saw her sitting on a rock staring out at the water beyond. He approached her and felt the first drops of rain on his skin.

"It's starting to rain, that'll be good for the greenery around here before the summer kicks in," he said as he plonked himself on the rock next to her.

She smiled at him before turning back to the waters. "I think I can see land," she said, "look over there where it seems to get darker," she pointed and Iwot followed her finger squinting across the blue expanse.

"I can't see anything Anika, I'm sorry," he said.

"You aren't looking hard enough that's all. I can see it, I know it's there," she replied, before jumping off of the rock and landing in the grass, "come on, let's go back, I want some of that boar."

Watching her leave, he smiled to himself. Deep down inside he hoped she would never find a way across the waters. He knew it was selfish but he hated the thought of never seeing her again.

That night, she sat around the fire with the rest of the tribe celebrating the successful hunt; dancing and singing to the drums bought at the festival. Anika's mind wandered as it always did and she glimpsed Shen out of the corner of her eye. He was what they called 'The wood master', as he could make anything out of wood. He was the one who selected the trees used to make the dugouts. She had spoken to him many times. After a moment, she got up and headed towards him. Around his legs, was one of his children who had been sent to bed but as yet was refusing to do so. Shen was too busy talking to take her right now and she seemed content to sit under his feet, chewing on the leather laces of his shoes.

"Hello, Shen. Masra misbehaving again?" she said with a smile. Masra looked up at her and grinned a big contagious smile.

Shen laughed, "as always. She'll learn one day how important sleep is but until then she can eat my shoelaces," he bent down and tickled her head. She responded with a giggle.

"I was wondering," Anika began, "Have you ever thought it possible to make a bigger boat?"

He looked at her for a moment pondering her question, "The thought has crossed my mind yes, Anika. The waters over there were not always there and I would like to see that land again, it was ripe and plentiful. Why do you ask?" he questioned.

Anika scratched her head a moment, sending bits of her hair flying around.

"I want to reach my father. We were separated when the giant wave hit and I cannot forget him, I won't forget him. Can you build a boat that will take me to him?" she spoke quickly and he almost struggled to understand her.

There was admiration in his eyes when he replied.

"It is possible, yes, but it would be a treacherous journey, maybe possible, maybe not," he said, looking at her, "you'd have to be prepared that you may never see your loved ones again," he concluded.

"I have already prepared myself for that," she said quietly thinking of Grenn, San and the children.

"Then it may well be possible. I've been waiting for a purpose to cross those waters, now I have one," he said, "I will need to put it to the tribe before we begin and it will take a while to build. We won't be leaving tomorrow."

She nodded trying her hardest not to allow the excitement to build up in her. She had moved one step closer again, one step closer to being reunited with her father.

Nineteen

It was almost a year later that the boat was ready. The tribe had met and voted and the majority of them agreed it was a good idea to try to trade with the people on the opposite land; find resources; branch out and form other tribes. Many were unaware that it was Anika's idea as the tribe's wise man decided that they were less likely to agree to the whims of a child.

The first step was to find a tree large enough to make the main bulk of the boat out of. Gre, who had told Anika of the giant wave he had seen back at the gathering, became a part of the building team. It took a journey of two days to find trunks of a lime tree with a wide enough circumference and also tall. Lime was used because it was the easiest to carve with the tools they possessed. Underneath the tree, a fire was lit to make it fall as it could sometimes take them days just to cut down a tree. They then needed to work out how to get it back to the tribe. Days of planning rolled into weeks of organising as they created a sled of sorts out of smaller tree trunks tied together with sinew, which the larger trunk was lifted onto using thirty men. This was then pulled by aurochs directed by the men.

Finally, they made it back to greetings from their tribe who were excited to see the sleds created. Anika was at the front.

"Wow, Iwot! Look at how they are pulling it?" she cried as they ran towards the group of men.

"It's impressive," he replied.

Over the coming months the most tedious task was undertaken, leaving the great trunks to dry out. Anika viewed them every day as she set about her daily tasks and tried not to get frustrated by how long it was taking after the initial excitement at the thought of returning.

"Anika, it's going to be a while before it's ready. Staring at it won't help," Iwot said to her one day.

"I know that stupid. You don't have to tell me the obvious," she stomped off towards the men who were standing around the trunks discussing the next step.

A few days later, she watched as they began to dig out the trunk with shells after burning off the bark where needed. Anika set to work helping them and was up early in the morning and late at night contributing to the making of the boats. After this, they shaped the bow and stern into points to ensure they would glide through the water smoothly.

"How much longer do you think?" Anika asked Shen when she noticed him once again staring at the boats pondering the next step.

"We need to strengthen the base then test it for leaks on the water. This can't be rushed Anika," he said.

"I know," She replied, "it's just.." she began, but couldn't finish as she thought about the last time she had seen her father.

Shen put his hand on her shoulder, "we will get there Anika."

"Thank you," she said.

"No, thank you. You've given me an excuse to try, I've been waiting for a reason to go."

Anika looked around and noticed in the dirt not far from where they were standing, Shen's daughter, she was drawing circles with a stick.

"What about your daughter, Shen? You will leave her behind?" Anika asked.

He followed her gaze and watched with a smile as she began to pile little stones on top of each other. "I am doing this for her Anika. To ensure we can survive, we need to start trading with other tribes, see what is out there so we can keep surviving. My children and my children's children and onwards for generations to come." He smiled again, then got down on his knees and stroked his child's head. Anika watched, once again reminded of her own father.

Finally, one day, Shen came to Anika and Iwot as they sat around their hut. Iwot was carving arrowheads whilst Anika was attempting to bend a stick she had whittled ready to use as a bow.

"How long do you think it will take to finish those?" he said pointing to the bow and arrows.

"I'm not sure," Iwot said as he ran his hand down the edge of the flint, "why do you ask?" he looked up curious.

Shen smiled, "because we leave tomorrow," he said.

Anika dropped her bow and stood up, "really?Tomorrow?" she questioned.

"Yes."

"Tomorrow?"

"Yes," Shen said laughing now.

"Oh my, that is fantastic. We need to get ready. Iwot, get up," she tugged his arm, "Iwot now," she said.

"Alright, alright, wow, not sure I actually want to go with you," he said with a wink at Shen.

That night, they packed up. None of them were sure how long the crossing would take or if they would even make it, so the packing was done reflectively as each of them thought about the people they had left behind and the journey that had brought them so far. Their main concern was water as even though they would be surrounded by it, they knew that drinking it would kill them. Many animal bladders were filled and tied at the top to be stored in the bottom of the boat. Food wasn't such a problem as they had a lot in storage. Meat had been salted and smoked, they had a good collection of nuts and green leaves plus acorn biscuits. Gre came up to her earlier in the night before it got too dark. Sitting down next to her, she watched as he bit off a piece of meat from the hare he had just finished cooking.

"Anika, if you ever return, will you come this way?" he asked, "I mean, I'd like it if you would come this way. To see you again would be, well it would be nice." he finished.

Anika smiled at this boy she had grown to love like a brother over the past year. "Yes Gre, for sure," she replied, "I cannot thank you enough for what you have done for me. Leading us here, then helping with the boat. I couldn't have done it without you and wouldn't have wanted to."

He put his hand on hers.

"Uh hmmm," coughed Iwot, as he deliberately interrupted the moment taking place.

Anika pulled her hand away, "Iwot?" she said.

"It's getting late, we need to be off at first light. You should get some sleep," he said.

"You're right, thank you Gre," she stood up and smiled at him before walking away from the fire and heading for her furs.

At first light, Iwot and Anika began to pack their supplies into the boat. A crowd had come to see them off but she couldn't see Gre, she wasn't sure why he wouldn't come to say goodbye, but her focus turned to the boat and its crew swiftly as she realised they were ready.

Iwot had taken front position and had his paddle ready. She sat herself in the boat next to him, removing her shoes as she waded into the water and climbed in. The other four crew members, one woman and three men, also got in the boat which seemed to sink precariously but stayed afloat. Anika looked to the sky which was changing from purple to blue as the sun rose. Birds flew above her head, circling as they raced one another and searched for fish. There was only a small amount of movement in the waters today, all seemed calm. Perfect conditions to sail on. Iwot turned to her.

"Ready?" he said.

Anika looked back one more time in the hope of seeing Gre but as hard as she stared, she couldn't see him. She turned back to Iwot and the journey beyond.

"I'm ready," she said.

And out across the blue waters, amongst friends and many memories, Anika continued on her perilous return to find her father.

Printed in Great Britain
by Amazon

43715878R00108